Tackling disadvantage

A 20-year enterprise

David Darton, Donald Hirsch and Jason Strelitz

The **Joseph Rowntree Foundation** has supported this project as part of its programme of research and innovative development projects, which it hopes will be of value to policy makers, practitioners and service users. The facts presented and views expressed in this report are, however, those of the authors and not necessarily those of the Foundation.

Joseph Rowntree Foundation
The Homestead
40 Water End
York YO30 6WP
Website: www.jrf.org.uk

First published 2003 by the Joseph Rowntree Foundation

ISBN 1 85935 091 7 (paperback)
1 85935 092 5 (pdf: available at www.jrf.org.uk)

A CIP catalogue record for this report is available from the British Library.

Designed by Adkins Design
Printed by Fretwells Ltd

Contents

Use of terms

This report uses:

'Poverty' to signify a lack of resources that prevents individuals and households from reaching an adequate standard of living.

'Disadvantage' to signify a wider set of difficulties preventing people from participating fully in society, including poverty but also, for example, limiting factors in one's life situation (such as a lack of skills), unequal levels of health and well-being associated with economic disadvantage, and discrimination.

'Social exclusion' to signify the processes which create disadvantage.

'Family' to signify a nuclear family including at least one dependent child.

'Household' to signify a single person or group of people living at the same address as their only or main residence, who either share one meal a day together or share the living accommodation (i.e. living room). This sometimes includes more than one **'nuclear'** economic unit (family, childless couple or single adult).

Income **'before housing costs'** or **'after housing costs'** as two alternative measures of household income. Both measure income after tax. After housing cost income also subtracts the amount that a household spends on rent and on mortgage interest. This makes it possible to compare disposable incomes. In this report 'after housing costs' is used as the preferred measure when available.

'Median income' as a measure of an income norm that is different from the conventional average or 'mean'. Rather than dividing total income by the number of households, it looks at the income of the household in the middle of the income distribution. Half of all households are above the median, half are below.

Foreword

The Joseph Rowntree Foundation has been taking stock of how its work relates to today's and tomorrow's social problems. This publication is part of this forward look to assess what issues we should be addressing now if we are to help prevent worsening social difficulties some twenty years hence.

Are the key themes for the Foundation's R&D still valid? What 'underlying causes of social evils' are we failing to address? What are the issues for social policy in the UK which need tackling today to prevent an escalation of emerging social problems tomorrow?

With our centenary approaching, the JRF Trustees initiated an internal review looking at the priorities and parameters for our work. This led us to consider the remits for the Research and Development Committees which Trustees have established to seek and sift proposals for new work. The key conclusion from this exercise was that the Foundation should continue to give a high priority to the two areas of concern with which we have been associated for so long: issues of 'place' and of 'poverty'.

Joseph Rowntree began his pioneering work in 1902 by starting the building of a strong, mixed-income, new community – not just to provide a better life for those from the slums of York, but also to create a place of good neighbourliness and mutual support. We are continuing to test the practicalities of housing and community ideas directly through our Housing Trust; and we have now also re-affirmed the centrality of 'place' – of housing and neighbourhoods – within our ongoing research work.

The other core JRF theme – 'poverty' – dates back to Seebohm Rowntree's first study in York, published in 1901. We remain committed to seeking objective measures of relative poverty to determine whether levels are rising or falling and to discover how best an impact can be made upon this most basic form of social disadvantage.

At the end of 2002, Trustees concluded that these themes should remain at the heart of the Foundation's work. A core R&D Committee for each will continue to advise the Trustees on how best we can deploy resources under these headings. (Other advisory committees will be created with time-limited programmes of work focused on specific subjects that will change over time.)

In a parallel exercise to this internal review, the Trustees instituted a forward look at emerging social concerns. A series of seminars and individual discussions were held in 2001/02, drawing on the input of academics, policy commentators, practitioners and other colleagues: these have provided an analysis of the likely problems which will face the UK in the 2020s. This work should help us draw out the kind of changes for today that might head off the problems of tomorrow.

The result of this programme is a collection of papers, providing insights into the problems and suggesting ways forward, which we are now publishing on our website. The material – with contributions from well-known journalists as well as academics – has been distilled into a series of chapters. *Tackling UK poverty and disadvantage in the twenty-first century: An exploration of the issues* can be downloaded from the JRF website bookshop (www.jrf.org.uk/bookshop/).

And, to draw on all this material, we asked three people to prepare a summary for use as a JRF Working Paper. The publication that follows is the outcome, prepared by David Darton (previously Director of Communications at the JRF and now with the Equal Opportunities Commission), Donald Hirsch (Special Adviser to the JRF and consultant to the OECD), and Jason Strelitz (formerly of the JRF, now at the LSE's Centre for the Analysis of Social Exclusion). We are enormously grateful to this team for pulling together this readable analysis: it contains suggestions for addressing the major social problems it describes.

Joseph Rowntree created our Foundation in December 1904 and Trustees have decided to celebrate our centenary in December 2004 with a major event on the themes of *poverty* and *place*. We hope that *Tackling disadvantage: A 20-year enterprise* will make a central contribution to the thinking before, after and at the JRF Centenary Conference. A hundred years on we continue to search for the causes of these social problems and to propose policy remedies which could – as Joseph Rowntree hoped – 'change the face' of this country.

Richard Best,
Director, JRF
January 2003

Introduction

On many measures the UK economy is successful and our average standard of living is one of the highest in the world. However, the proportion of people living in relative poverty rose dramatically after the mid 1970s and since the mid 1990s has remained at stubbornly high levels despite initiatives aimed at reducing it.

Through its research over the past few years, the Joseph Rowntree Foundation has found strong evidence of the hardship caused by poverty and associated disadvantage. In particular, it has found that a large proportion of the population are unable to afford the products and activities which the majority feel are essential, and that many disadvantaged people have difficulties in accessing adequate services.

It is clear that only long-term, sustained action on a range of fronts can adequately tackle these difficulties. Over the past two years, therefore, the Foundation has consulted a wide range of experts (listed in the Appendix on page 48) about the broad approaches that might help us tackle poverty and associated disadvantage in a major way over the next 20 years. The objective of this exercise was primarily to inform the Foundation's research priorities. But in mapping out some of the critical issues, it has identified some areas that need particular attention. This report aims to share this 'map' as a contribution to debating what should take priority in tackling poverty and disadvantage over the next 20 years.

The report is concerned more with economic well-being than has been traditional for the Foundation. Part I maps out the nature of poverty – who is affected by it and some of the major trends affecting it. It rehearses the reasons why it is important to tackle the poverty that exists and the broad economic feasibility of doing so. It concludes that it will be a tough but affordable mission and that four principles will need to underlie a broad-based strategy that increases both opportunity and support for those who are potentially disadvantaged. These principles are: to increase the extent to which poorer households and communities can benefit from the market economy; to ensure an adequate floor income for everyone that relates to what society considers to be the essentials of modern living; to ensure access to other resources necessary to this, such as housing and care; and to ensure that in the implementation of policies, there is no discrimination.

The last of these cuts across all areas, is a very large topic and not a focus of this report, since this general mapping exercise does not propose the details of policy implementation. However, with respect to the other principles, our consultations have suggested some particular areas that need attention. Part II contains short four-page sections setting out the issues in six areas. The first two pages in each case consider the problems that need to be tackled and the second pair the long-term goals that policy needs to adopt and some of the consequent directions it might take, illustrating some of these with examples of possible policy as a stimulus for further thinking.

The first of our overall principles, increasing the capacity of people and communities to benefit from the market economy, can be pursued across a range of policy areas. In this report we identify in particular the importance of focusing education resources on the most disadvantaged, of complementing this with more general support for children and families, and of improving the capacity of disadvantaged areas – whole regions as well as smaller localities – to prosper. In respect of ensuring an adequate floor income, the second principle, the chapter on income suggests how policy may strengthen support without relying excessively on means-testing. Finally, in respect of improving access to non-monetary resources, the third principle, our consultations have confirmed that two areas that the Foundation has been researching for a long time are critical priorities given current trends: an adequate supply of housing, and access to long-term care. These are dealt with in the final two chapters of Part II, where some firm recommendations for policy directions reflect the Foundation's long involvement in these areas.

In some ways the task of navigating the broad map set out in this report feels daunting. However, with clear-sighted action over the long term, substantial progress is possible. Above all, we argue that the UK's prosperous economy can afford to tackle poverty and disadvantage if the political will to do so can be built and sustained.

Part I

Overview of the problem and principles for action

Poverty: The past 20 years

The poorest groups missed out on the economic growth of the 1980s. In the 1990s their incomes grew modestly, along with the rest of the population…

Figure 1 **Growth in real incomes, by place in income distribution**

Source: Office for National Statistics (2002)

Note: Each line on the above graph shows income growth at a particular point in the distribution. For example a person who is poorer than exactly 90% of the population is at the 10th percentile.

…the result has been a near doubling of the number of people in relative poverty, to a plateau of 13–14 million on incomes below 60 per cent of the median…

Figure 2 **Population with household incomes below 60 per cent of median (after housing costs)**

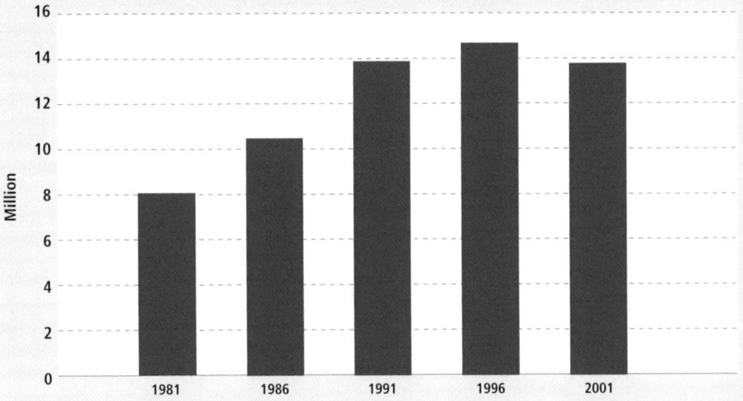

Million: 16, 14, 12, 10, 8, 6, 4, 2, 0

1981, 1986, 1991, 1996, 2001

Source: Office for National Statistics (2001a)

…which is one of the highest rates in Europe.

Figure 3 **Poverty in OECD countries – percentage of population with household incomes below 60 per cent of median**

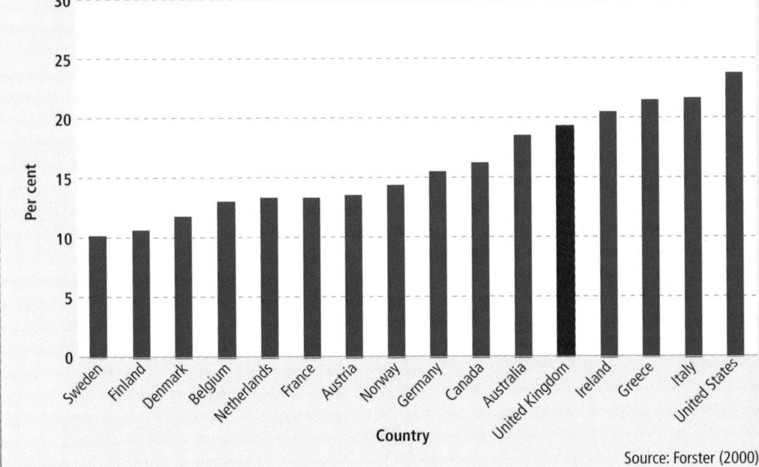

Source: Forster (2000)

Note that due to data availability, Figure 2 uses income after housing costs, and Figure 3 before housing costs. See explanation of terms, page 4.

Tackling poverty and disadvantage: A 20-year enterprise

Poverty and disadvantage constitute a scar on the UK's economic success...
Life has become more prosperous for the majority of British people over the past two decades. Most people enjoy greatly enhanced material living standards and leisure activities. Since 1981 a household in the middle of the income distribution has had nearly a 50 per cent rise in income, after inflation. However, the poorest section of the population has fallen behind. Their incomes have risen more slowly than average, leaving more in relative poverty (see Figures 1 and 2). This trend has been much more pronounced than in most other European countries, whose poverty rates are substantially lower (Figure 3).

Alongside rising poverty, there have been increases in other forms of disadvantage, such as poorer health among worse-off groups, and homelessness. In some cases whole communities have been falling further and further behind.

...and are exacerbated by ongoing pressures...
This deterioration has been influenced by a wide range of social, economic and demographic trends which continue to put pressure on disadvantaged groups. They include:

- the long-term loss of jobs in manufacturing industries
- a decline in the demand for unskilled labour, combined with the growing importance of skills
- new patterns of living that have broken down important family bonds and support networks
- a growth in the proportion of older people
- a growth in the number of single person households, with a corresponding increase in pressures on housing.

...but could be effectively tackled in the next 20 years with a concerted effort.
A major challenge facing the UK is to obliterate this scar on Britain's economic and social landscape over the next 20 years, while ensuring that the momentum of recent economic growth is sustained. This report argues that, despite many adverse factors, such an ambition is realisable, given the will. It will require action on a range of fronts, following some underlying principles designed to give priority to the needs of disadvantaged groups, without ignoring the factors required for general economic development.

Poverty rates are the key indicator in this wider assault on disadvantage
Poverty in Britain is inextricably intertwined with disadvantages in health, housing, education and other aspects of life. It is hard for people who lack resources to take advantage of the opportunities available to the rest of society. People move in and out of poverty, but the great majority of those who are poor at any one moment face some form of persisting low income.

Because of the association of low income with wider disadvantage, a central challenge for the next 20 years is to minimise the number of people living below a defined level of income, relative to the average. For reasons given below, this report proposes a minimum threshold of 60 per cent of median. Together with the principles set out in the report, this gives society a ready measure of progress along the long road to tackling disadvantage.

The factors behind poverty and disadvantage in the twenty-first century

The new labour market

Figure 4 **New jobs have been in skilled and service occupations...**
Projected employment change 1981–2010

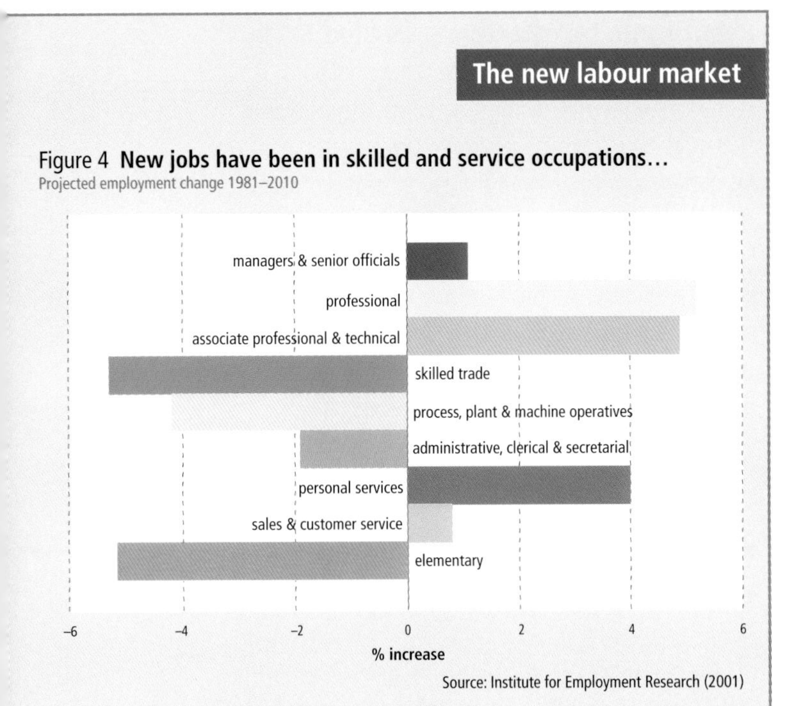

Source: Institute for Employment Research (2001)

Figure 5 **...and rises in pay have been concentrated in the best-paid jobs.**
Increase in full-time male wages (in real terms; 1980 = 100)

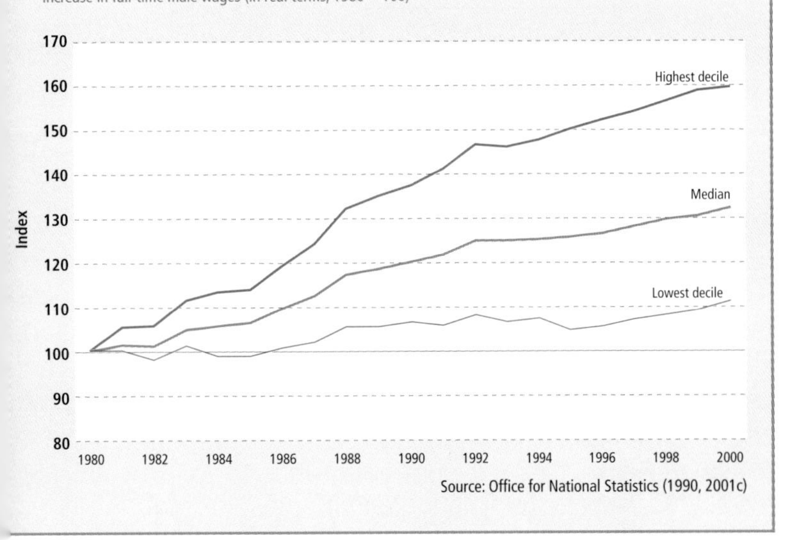

Source: Office for National Statistics (1990, 2001c)

Why does a prosperous country such as the UK find it so hard to eradicate widespread poverty and its social consequences? The theory that rising prosperity should 'trickle down' to the poor has not on the whole proven correct. In general, worse-off people in recent years have seen their living standards either stagnate, or rise much more slowly than the average. The result has been a growth in inequalities and in associated disadvantage.

Behind these widening differences lie a variety of long-term economic, demographic and social trends that have influenced developments in the past 20 years, and continue to do so. They include in particular:

Labour market trends: New jobs, wage inequalities and exclusion

The changing occupational structure (Figure 4) has widened the gap in wages between more and less skilled jobs, and has contributed to an uneven distribution of employment across geographic areas and across different households.

As the demand for skilled, educated labour grows, a greater premium is being placed on higher skills. Wages for the lowest paid workers have barely increased at all in 20 years, whereas for those near the top of the earnings distribution they rose 60 per cent in real terms (Figure 5).

A recurring theme of this report is the concentration of job opportunities in certain geographic areas. But, in addition, the way in which they are distributed among households with adults of working age has undergone important changes. In the last quarter of the twentieth century, employment rates for women rose from 58 per cent to 70 per cent, while those for men declined from 92 per cent to 80 per cent (Office for National Statistics 2001a). The new female workers are mostly in households with a working male. Therefore, the proportion of households with nobody working rose sharply from 8 per cent in 1979 to 17 per cent in 2000 (Dickens et al. 2001).

Pay and employment rates have become more unequal across skill groups, communities and households. The result is a concentration of disadvantage among certain households with low skills, whose members are unable to find work, or who are obliged to work in low-paid and often unstable jobs.

Geographic trends: Polarising communities

Recent years have seen a net migration out of the major cities and conurbations and into smaller towns, suburban greenfield developments and rural areas (Bate et al. 2000). This migration has been led by more prosperous individuals, leaving many poorer people behind in cities with fewer jobs and a declining infrastructure. Table 1 shows an example of the wide differences in economic inactivity currently experienced in different areas of Britain.

Table 1 **Economic inactivity in contrasting places** (percentage of working age population who are economically inactive)

	Male	Female
Knowsley	28.1	44.1
Merthyr Tydfil	27.7	43.2
Milton Keynes	8.2	18.3
Swindon	6.1	17.7

Source: National Statistics (2002)

Growing differences across and within regions cause a variety of problems in different parts of the country. In the crowded south, the lack of housing both to rent and to buy creates particular hardship for the poorest groups. They are less likely to be able to exercise choice about the quality or location of their home, and for some people a lack of housing opportunities leads to homelessness. In the north, large clusters of poor areas suffer from a fundamental lack of wealth generation, with some parts of cities being virtually abandoned.

Demographic trends and the growth of vulnerable groups

The UK population is changing in a number of ways that can lead to increases in disadvantage among certain groups.

Life expectancy is increasing, and the over-65s will rise from 16 per cent to 20 per cent of the population over the next 20 years.[1] Pensions need to sustain older people for longer than in the past. The growing number who are very old is already creating a crisis in the quality and availability of care. In both cases, poorer groups are the most vulnerable.

Marriage rates have fallen, divorce and cohabitation have risen, and many women are having children later: the result is a much greater variety of households. In some cases, this has eroded traditional means of economic support, and increased vulnerability, particularly among families with children.

Minority ethnic populations are growing as a percentage of the total. Some of these populations remain particularly vulnerable to disadvantage, with high poverty rates exacerbated by discrimination.[2]

The rate of immigration has risen in recent years, and forecasts of the future migration rate have recently grown (GAD 2002). The immigrant population includes both the very rich and the very poor: although some people come to the UK, especially London, to work in high-income jobs, at the other end a relatively high proportion of new immigrants arrive with little and face considerable hardship.

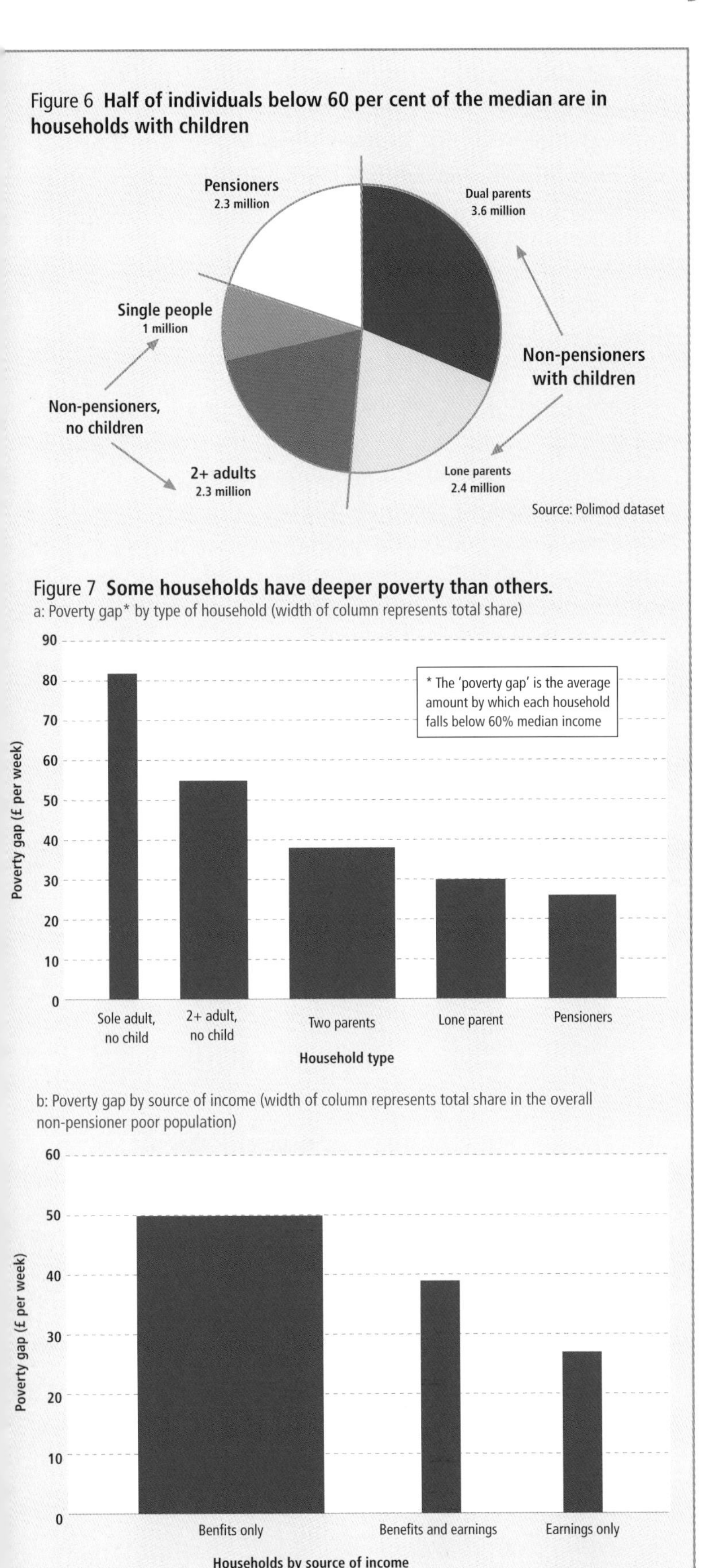

Figure 6 **Half of individuals below 60 per cent of the median are in households with children**

Source: Polimod dataset

Figure 7 **Some households have deeper poverty than others.**

a: Poverty gap* by type of household (width of column represents total share)

b: Poverty gap by source of income (width of column represents total share in the overall non-pensioner poor population)

Source: Polimod dataset

Families have replaced pensioners as the largest group on low incomes...

Thirty years ago, almost half of individuals living in households with low incomes were pensioners. Today, fewer than a quarter are pensioners, and around half are children and their parents (Figure 6).

This is not because of a great reduction in the proportion of pensioners who are poor, but because of a sharp rise in the poverty rates of families with children. Today, a child has a 1 in 3 chance of being in a household with below 60 per cent median income, compared with a 1 in 7 chance in 1979 (Department for Work and Pensions 2002a).

Another way of looking at the distribution of poverty among various groups is to consider not just the numbers below a threshold but the average 'depth' of their poverty in terms of how far incomes are below the threshold.[3] Figure 7a shows that even though there are, for example, more pensioners than single people without children living in poor households, the 'poverty gap' is on average over three times as high for the latter than the former. This is quite simply because pensioners have a Minimum Income Guarantee that takes claimants to an income not far below 60 per cent of the median; Income Support for single people is much lower. Figure 7b confirms that 70 per cent of poor people rely on benefits only and these households are poorer than those in which there is some employment.

...but a range of overlapping groups are affected by poverty...

Although low income can be used as a rough indicator of disadvantage, in practice the situation of different groups on similar incomes varies widely. For example, a pensioner having to survive for 20 or 30 years on a low income is in a different situation from someone who is temporarily out of work and may only have low income for a few weeks or months. A number of groups suffering poverty, and vulnerable to wider disadvantage, give particular cause for concern.

Lone parents are the family group that have the highest risk of low income: about half have incomes below 60 per cent of the median. Their dual responsibility for both caring for their children and providing family income puts them in a particularly difficult position, which can be compounded by critical social attitudes.

Workless households, excluding pensioners, contain nearly half of individuals living in poverty in the UK. For families with children, being out of work is almost a guarantee of being poor – 90 per cent are below the threshold. In general, households depending on benefits have a greater chance of poverty than in the past, with basic Income Support providing only an eighth of average earnings, compared with a fifth in 1981 (Department for Work and Pensions 2002b).

People with low qualifications have higher than average chances of being poor, and face the prospect of recurring poverty.

Social housing tenants comprise one-fifth of all households, but one half of all households on low incomes. Social housing has become a last resort for many disadvantaged people, who have the least choice about where they live. This has led to concentrations of poverty, which can be associated with other difficulties such as lack of private sector investment, poor services and poor infrastructure. In turn disadvantaged people in these areas often find it difficult to improve their situation because of limited access to opportunities for work, education and training.

Members of certain *minority ethnic groups* have a greater than average chance both of poverty and disadvantage. Strikingly, those with any given qualification level have over twice as much chance of being unemployed as equally qualified white people (Department for Education and Employment 1999).

Disabled people have a high chance of being poor, despite needing extra resources to cope with their disabilities. A group with particularly high chances of being poor are disabled parents, who do not receive the support they need.

Women of course constitute a highly varied group, but overall are much more likely than men to be in low-income households. A particular issue with changing demographic trends is the inability of many women to build up sufficient pension entitlements to keep them out of poverty in retirement, the average duration of which has lengthened with increased life expectancy.

Pensioner poverty remains an important issue, despite an income guarantee aiming to prevent pensioners from falling into deep poverty. This guarantee remains below the level estimated by the independent Family Budget Unit to be sufficient to meet basic needs, and the inability of most pensioners to enhance their incomes by working makes poverty among this group potentially more serious in its consequences.

...creating hardship that the majority of the public find unacceptable.

Does it matter that all these groups of people risk having low incomes, relative to the average, given that overall living standards are rising? There are many debates to be had about the importance of absolute and relative poverty. What is indisputable is that a large section of the British population is unable to afford things that the general public consider to be essential.

Successive Joseph Rowntree Foundation surveys of deprivation have looked at how many people are unable to afford items that the majority of the public say are necessary and believe that people in Britain should not have to do without. The proportion of adults lacking at least three such necessities rose from 14 per cent in 1983 to 21 per cent in 1990 and 24 per cent in 1999 (Mack and Lansley 1983; Gordon and Pantazis 1997; Gordon et al. 2000).

In the light of such widespread deprivation, measured objectively by the standards of modern Britain, it is clear that today's levels of poverty and disadvantage do indeed matter.

The central challenge: Reversing the growth in relative poverty

Tackling relative poverty is important for everyone...

At the heart of the task of tackling disadvantage in twenty-first century Britain is making sure that the poorest groups share in the nation's growing prosperity. Over the past 20 years, they have fallen behind. Over the next 20, it is possible to reverse this by ensuring that a disproportionate share of the fruits of further growth go to the least advantaged.

There is a growing consensus about the need to tackle relative poverty for three main reasons:

Social justice It is the mark of a civilized society that increasing prosperity is used to the benefit of all citizens, and that everyone has an acceptable minimum standard of living.

Economic prosperity Poverty and disadvantage limit the economic potential of people who could contribute positively.

Strengthening civil society Exclusion from the mainstream can cause alienation and a breakdown of civic ties, with potentially severe consequences for everyone.

...and the best single benchmark is the number of households on below 60 per cent of median income...

Following extensive consultation, we believe that the proportion of the population in households with less than 60 per cent of median income (adjusted according to family type) constitutes the best single measure to monitor progress in eradicating poverty.

This is inevitably an arbitrary figure. However, there are good reasons, first for choosing a figure, second for relating it to the median and third for setting this particular level.

Having a single, relative measure to which politicians and the public relate can help sustain the priority of poverty eradication, as is already apparent in the quest to end child poverty.

Choosing a median rather than a mean income threshold helps relate poverty to the norms of ordinary people – it is a more natural definition of a 'middling' income. The number of people below a percentage of mean income can rise solely as the result of the rising incomes of the rich, which has limited relevance to the standards and aspirations of poor groups.

The 60 per cent figure, while not a scientific definition of poverty, is the most widely recognised international poverty threshold, allowing ready comparisons with similar countries. Moreover, it is close to the income required to afford a 'low cost but acceptable' budget. This has been calculated by the Family Budget Unit, based on the cost of some very basic items, although excluding some items such as tobacco and debt payments (see Figure 8). (In practice many poor households who are struggling to make ends meet accumulate considerable debt.) This shows that, in general terms, 60 per cent of median is the kind of income that households need to avoid severe hardship.

Figure 8 **Poverty thresholds for two adults and two children**

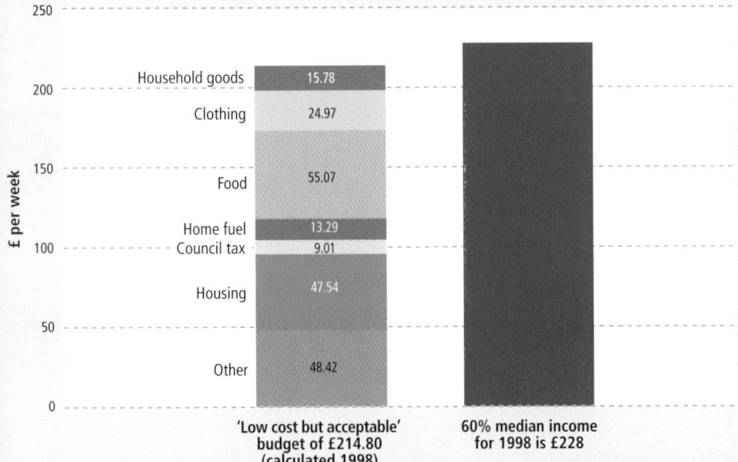

250
200
150
100
50
0
£ per week

Household goods 15.78
Clothing 24.97
Food 55.07
Home fuel 13.29
Council tax 9.01
Housing 47.54
Other 48.42

'Low cost but acceptable' budget of £214.80 (calculated 1998)

60% median income for 1998 is £228

Source: Parker (1998)

...so a basic principle is to minimise this number over the next 20 years...

It would be unrealistic to aim to ensure tomorrow that nobody has to live on incomes below 60 per cent median. However, over the long term it is possible to erode the numbers in poverty so defined. Two key principles for the next 20 years are:

- to minimise the number of people with incomes below 60 per cent median

- for those who do fall short of this threshold at any point during their lives, to reduce the amount of time spent on such incomes.

These twin principles do not constitute targets in the sense of wholly eradicating poverty in a given period, but are based on the judgement that the problem can be largely conquered and, more importantly, that one can move continuously in this direction. It would be unrealistic to expect progress every year, in good times and in bad, but a key aim is a cycle on cycle reduction in the number below 60 per cent median – that the number should fall continuously from one economic cycle to the next.

...which is a tough but affordable mission. Some of the long-term trends noted above make the combating of relative poverty an uphill struggle. It would be foolish to pretend that the task is easy. However, it is certainly affordable.

As a starting point, the Foundation has commissioned work to calculate how much of the growth of the next 20 years might be needed to bring today's poor households up to the threshold. If the economy grows at the same rate as in the past 20 years, total growth will be over £500 billion. Only a small proportion of this, less than £25 billion, would be needed to close the poverty gap completely. This would require the poorest groups to experience the same rate of rises in living standards as those enjoyed by the most affluent in the 1980s, and the incomes of the rest of the population to grow only marginally more slowly than in the past five years (see Figures 9 to 11).

In practice, the amount that needs to be redistributed could be somewhat more or somewhat less than this. Less redistribution will be needed if more people move into work, and if people in low-paying jobs become more productive and better paid. On the other hand if employment and pay patterns were to remain the same while income support levels increased, higher tax credits may also be needed to keep in-work incomes sufficiently above out-of-work incomes, maintaining work incentives. So the true cost is uncertain. But even if it were 50 per cent higher than estimated above, the country would need to give up only about £1 for every extra £15 of economic growth.

Growth: who benefits? Real income growth by quintile

Figure 9 **Over most of the past 20 years, incomes grew much faster for richer groups...**

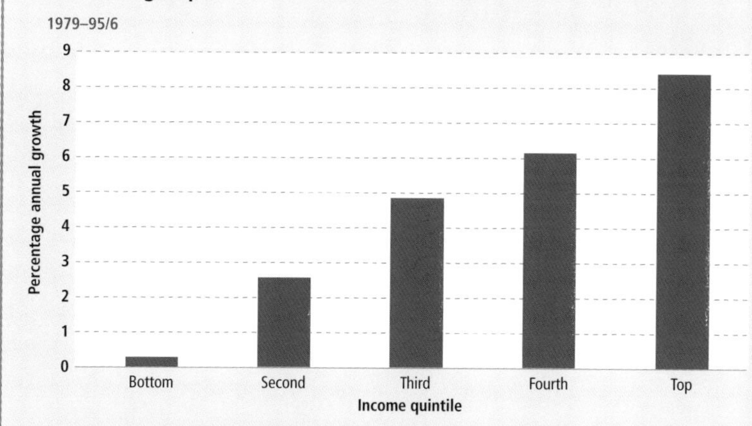

Figure 10 **...but more recently there has been steady, moderate growth across the board...**

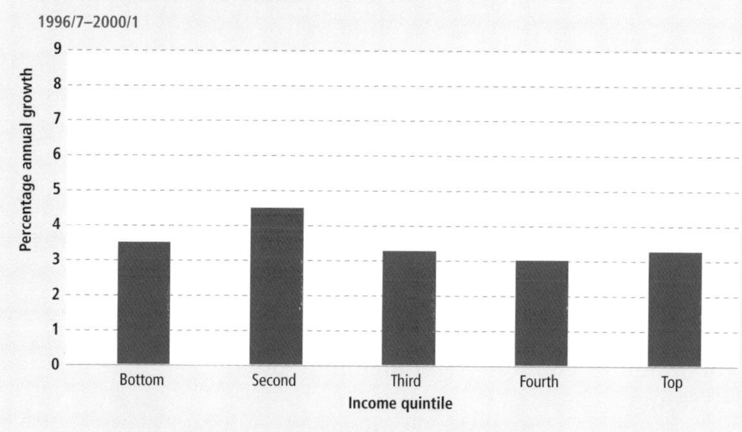

Figure 11 **...and with the same overall rate of economic growth over the next 20 years, skewed to the poor, it could bring them above 60 per cent median, while other groups maintain modest rises.**

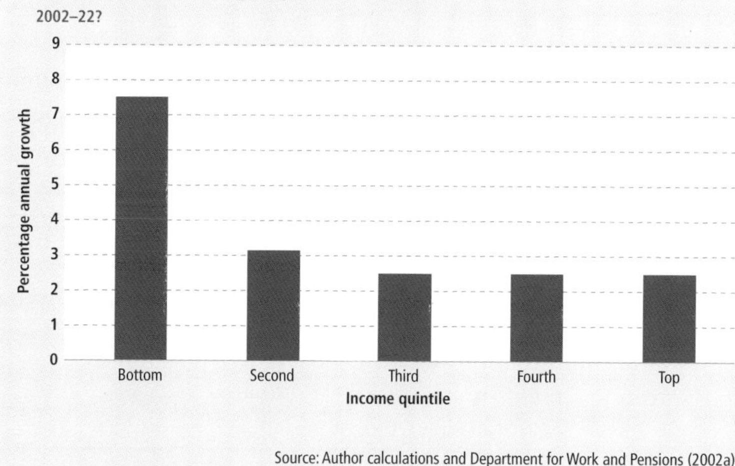

Source: Author calculations and Department for Work and Pensions (2002a)

A broad-based strategy combining opportunity and support

Improved incomes must be linked with a broader assault on other forms of disadvantage...
Every year the Joseph Rowntree Foundation publishes key indicators of poverty and social exclusion. While poverty rates and the incidence of various types of disadvantage can go up or down, one thing remains broadly constant. Poorer groups are more likely than average to suffer a range of other disadvantages, such as poor health and fear (as well as incidence) of crime (Rahman et al. 2001). Moreover, a wide range of disadvantages in childhood and youth – from mental health problems to low educational attainment – are experienced more by people with worse-off parents. Therefore, strategies to fight poverty and to combat wider social disadvantage need to go hand in hand.

A single coherent strategy needs to be based on some basic principles, based around providing conditions that allow people who are presently disadvantaged to prosper. The four principles below aim to get to the roots of disadvantage, by tackling the factors that have held people back as well as guaranteeing access to resources more directly.

...by helping people to achieve their potential...
A strategy to tackle disadvantage must start by aiming not just to rescue people when they fail but to help them to succeed. ***Principle 1*** is therefore ***to increase the capacity of poorer households and communities to gain from the market economy***. This will both help the individuals concerned and benefit society more widely, making it easier to reconcile a focus on disadvantage with a continuation of economic growth.

...creating an adequate income floor...
However much the potential of disadvantaged groups is improved over the long term, redistribution of income will also be required, both to enable people to develop their own capacity and to protect the needs of those whom the market fails. ***Principle 2*** is therefore ***to ensure an adequate floor income that relates to what as a society we believe are the necessities of contemporary living***. The policy priority proposed here is to minimise the number of people in households with below 60 per cent of median income.

...giving access to other resources...
Shortage of income, however, is not the only aspect of relative poverty. Severe disadvantage also occurs for some because of a shortage of other resources, particularly healthcare, personal care and housing. In such areas, poorer groups are particularly dependent on being able to access adequate public services, and lack the means to shop around for private alternatives. ***Principle 3*** is therefore ***to ensure that all, particularly relatively poor people and those living in multiply deprived areas, have access to adequate healthcare, personal care, housing and other essential services***.

...and combating discrimination.
In some cases, greater risk of poverty and disadvantage is associated with certain personal characteristics – gender, race, disability, sexual orientation, religion, and age. Under European legislation discrimination on these grounds will be outlawed, but only in relation to employment. This needs to be considered in relation to the provision of services and to the implementation of all policies aimed at tackling disadvantage. ***Principle 4*** is therefore ***to ensure that in the implementation of policies aimed at tackling disadvantage there is no discrimination on the grounds of gender, race, disability, sexual orientation, religion or age.*** (This principle cuts across the policy areas analysed below, and is not dealt with in any detail as we do not discuss specific implementation issues in this report.)

This report argues for giving systematic priority to the disadvantaged
Part II of this report looks at how these principles can be applied in some specific policy areas. An over-arching priority, which can be applied to any policy area, is to give a high priority to the tackling

of disadvantage, without ignoring more general policy requirements.

In some cases, where disadvantaged people have been held back by problems that affect society as a whole, policies to improve the situation generally will help them. For example, a mismatch in housing demand and supply in different parts of the country creates difficulties for all social groups, but with worse-off ones experiencing the greatest hardship. Overall improvements in supply would help homeless people as well as more affluent households. A regeneration of declining communities would both create new opportunities for their residents and avoid some of the wider economic difficulties that result from an over-concentration of prosperity in certain parts of the country.

In other cases, there is a need to think much more radically about reordering priorities to help the worst off. For example, how will the large amount of extra public resources allocated to education be deployed? So far, the skewing of resources to help disadvantaged groups in education has been small relative to overall spending, which is distributed largely on the basis of fixed amounts per pupil. A greater concentration of extra resources on tackling disadvantage could start to improve things for those who have hitherto gained little from the country's growing educational success.

This report proposes some long-term objectives and principles that society can sign up to, in a more conscious attempt to tackle some of its long-standing social problems. Such principles cannot determine every policy decision, but can serve to give a sense of direction, over a sustained period. The most tangible of these proposals is a new compass for tackling poverty: a single indicator (the number below 60 per cent of median income) of whether progress is being made, that ideally would become as important to governments as economic growth or unemployment rates. By heading in the right direction, progress can be made towards completing even the longest of journeys.

Income and disadvantage

Figure 12 **Poorer groups are less likely to do well at school...**

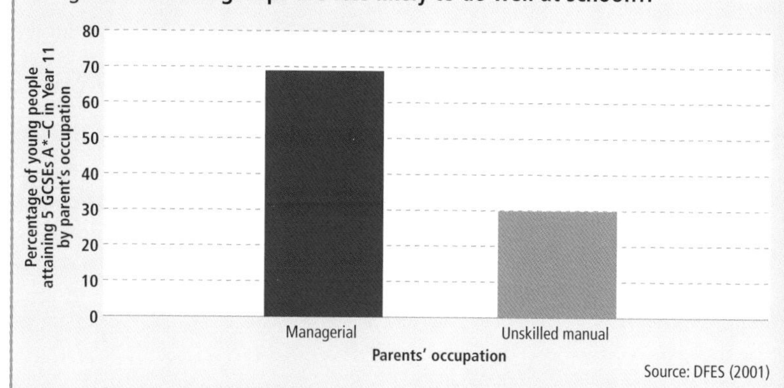

Source: DFES (2001)

Figure 13 **...are more likely to fear crime...**

Source: Home Office (2000)

Figure 14 **...and are more likely to have mental health problems as children.**

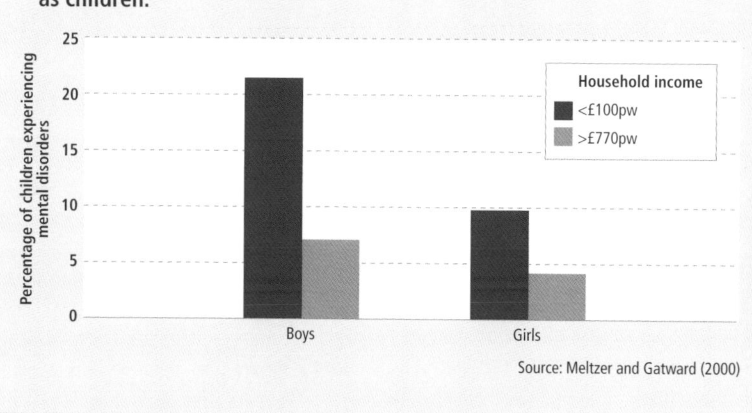

Source: Meltzer and Gatward (2000)

Part II

Tackling disadvantage in six areas of policy

Part I of this report ended by setting out basic principles for tackling poverty and disadvantage. Part II demonstrates how some of these principles can be applied in some key areas of public policy. It does not aim to be comprehensive, but rather to show the basis on which the principles can be translated into some long-term policy goals. Although it illustrates these with reference to certain specific policy examples, its aim is not to make policy recommendations but to provide a compass for the long-term development of policy in these areas.

The analysis starts by considering education, the area for which the first principle of helping people to achieve their potential is most directly relevant. It then looks at three areas in which a lack of opportunity has held people back, although improved opportunities need to be combined with direct support for those who suffer disadvantage. These cover, respectively, family poverty, regional disadvantage and income adequacy. The last two areas are specific cases in which the third principle, of giving access to particular basic resources other than income, are particularly important: housing and long-term care.

1 Education: Social inequalities matter more than ever

While educational opportunities expand, unequal outcomes by social background persist...

In the past 20 years, participation in education in the UK has expanded dramatically. More students are staying on at school, and higher education has expanded from serving a small elite to enrolling over a third of the youth population, one of the highest rates in the world. Yet the majority of those in the most disadvantaged groups have been left behind by this improvement.

As they approach the end of compulsory education at age 15, UK students now show reading and other relevant skills that, overall, are well above the average for similar countries (Figure 15). Yet the UK also has some of the greatest differences between students whose parents are well educated and in good jobs, and students from less advantaged backgrounds (OECD 2001). This helps to explain why 1 in 4 UK students still fail to get a single GCSE at grade C or above – the basic qualification associated with continuing in education or getting a promising job with good pay, conditions and development opportunities. By age 17, the failure of the UK system to provide for this minority is showing very clearly in one of the highest rates of early departure from education and training among OECD countries (Figure 16).

The failure of educational improvements to remove disadvantages determined by home background can be seen clearly in Figures 17 and 18. Half of all students are now achieving at least five good GCSEs, but in schools with a high concentration of students from low-income families, typically only 1 in 5 achieve this result (National Literacy Trust 1995). Similarly, while higher education has now become the norm for children from professional backgrounds, only a small minority of children from manual backgrounds benefit from it. In later life, shortfalls in initial education are compounded, as those with lower initial attainment are far less likely to develop their skills through continuous education and training.

Within certain geographical and ethnic communities, there is a particular concentration of disadvantage, especially for boys. Among African, Caribbean and Bangladeshi boys, only 22 per cent obtain at least five GCSEs at grade C or above.[4]

Education – the problem

Figure 15 **Although 15-year-olds in the UK perform well on average in the latest international tests...**

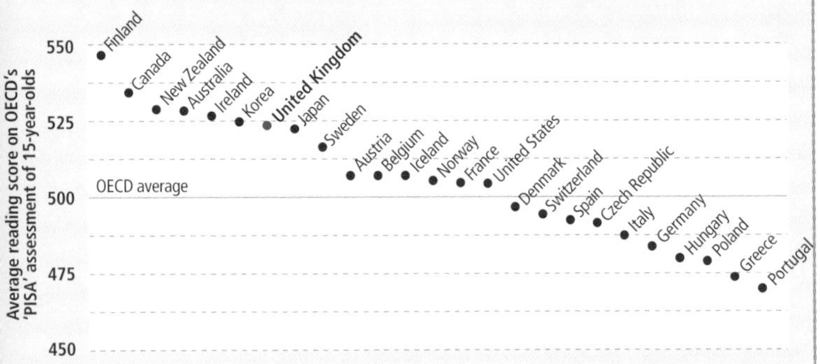

Source: OECD (2001)

Figure 16 **...fewer than in other countries stay on at school.**

Source: OECD (1998)

...this matters more than ever before, because skills are essential...

Tackling educational inequalities and low attainment are essential in any strategy to tackle disadvantage. For individuals, the ability to obtain and progress in good jobs is the single most important way of avoiding poverty. Today, such progress depends more than ever before on having appropriate skills. A decline in traditional industries is associated not just with fewer manual and unskilled jobs, but also for example with reduced demand for certain routine white-collar 'semi-skilled' work. The rise in the importance of service industries makes various interpersonal skills more important, while generic skills such as communication, numeracy, literacy, and information technology skills are needed across a wide range of jobs.

A lack of skills can affect communities as well as individuals: in many parts of the UK it will be impossible to generate more jobs without a greater number of skilled people. Britain's major cities have seen employment decline, and new jobs are often filled by people commuting from outside the area, because local residents lack necessary qualifications. In some other areas, such as former coalfields, the low skill base has contributed to a lack of inward investment, and to persistently low labour demand.[5]

...but to tackle this problem, some complex, deep-rooted causes must be addressed.

The persistence of low educational attainment and its concentration among people from disadvantaged backgrounds result from the interaction of a wide range of factors, including home background, school intake and school quality.

Home background Research shows consistent links between various aspects of home background and achievement at school. The level of education of one's own parents is significant, as is the degree to which parents take an interest in their children's education and give them active support. Early years development is strongly influenced by family life, health and nutrition (Danziger and Waldfogel 2000). Over and above such factors, the experience of poverty itself is strongly associated with low attainment.

Two implications follow from these findings. First, potentially the most powerful 'educational' policy is one that tackles social and economic disadvantage (Robinson 1997). Second, the benefit of ongoing emotional support, encouragement and reinforcement of the value of education should not be underestimated. This can help students to acquire attitudes that help them to develop and deploy human capital (i.e. acquire and use skills) effectively throughout their lives. So schools' relationships with families can be crucial.

School intake There is clear evidence that peer groups have a strong impact on the educational attainment of their members. This derives not just from more able students learning from each other, but also from the transmission of values and behaviours. Where more advantaged or able students are concentrated in some schools or classes, and less advantaged students in others, achievement is potentially polarised (Robertson and Symonds 1996). Specifically, geographical concentration of disadvantage, for example on large public housing estates, can impact on local schools (Clark et al. 1999).

School quality Repeated studies and evidence from OFSTED show that even schools with similar intakes can have very different results. These are associated with differences in leadership, teaching and the learning environment. The importance of quality relative to intake should not be exaggerated: in the present system, even high quality schools with a large number of students from disadvantaged backgrounds have below average results. However, evidence shows that given extra opportunities, for example much smaller classes, the performance of such schools can be lifted more rapidly (Molnar et al. 1999).

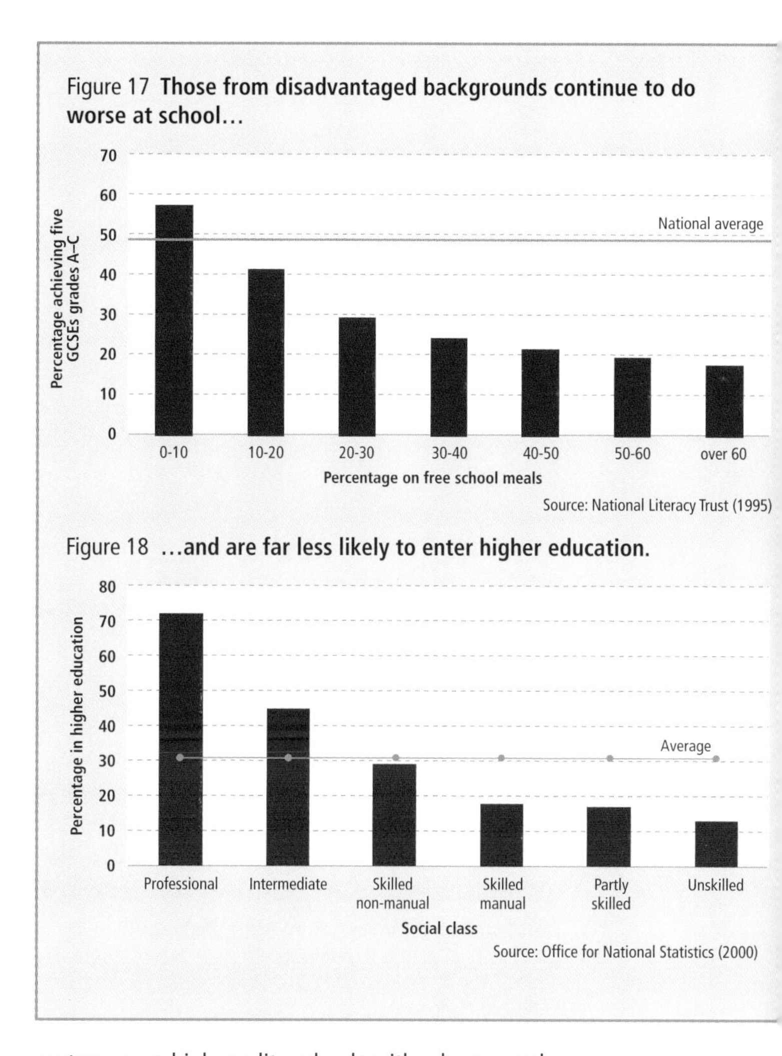

Tackling education: Focusing on disadvantage

In order to give people from disadvantaged backgrounds a better start in life, it is not enough to improve the education system generally; specific needs have to be addressed.

Long-term policy goals

- Focus resources and attention on helping disadvantaged students realise their potential.
- Tackle concentrations of disadvantage.

Present policy approaches…

The present Government has recognised the importance of persistent educational disadvantage, and developed a broad policy agenda to tackle it. It seeks in particular:

- as part of its war on child poverty, to focus on the early development of young children from disadvantaged backgrounds
- to improve the school system's ability to ensure that everybody acquires basic skills, for example through the literacy and numeracy hours in primary schools – which appear to be narrowing the gap in achievement between students from different social backgrounds
- to create closer links with families, for example by requiring schools to provide more information, and by making home–school agreements obligatory. For disadvantaged families, Sure Start seeks to involve parents actively in their children's education, on an ongoing basis
- to give extra resources to disadvantaged communities through area-based initiatives. Following the curtailment of Education Action Zones, Excellence in Cities has injected an extra £300m into a wide variety of programmes aimed at improving attainment in inner city schools.

…and their limitations.

Such efforts may be insufficient, in light not just of increased poverty and area polarisation, but also of features of the education system that are systematically disadvantaging people from poorer backgrounds.

The combined impact of school choice, league tables and school funding based directly on student numbers encourages secondary schools to focus resources on students close to crossing the five GCSE attainment threshold on which headline student performance is based, rather than on lower performers. It also encourages schools, where possible, to seek to enrol more privileged students, sowing the seeds of increased segregation (Hallgarten 2001).

Further factors cause a concentration of less advantaged students in particular schools, including residential concentrations and the interaction between house prices and the quality and results of local schools (Gibbons and Machin 2001). Such segregation matters because of the proven impact of peer group influences on educational inequality.

The fact that people from poorer backgrounds are more likely to go to schools where both student results and school quality is below average is also significant. One in 7 students in inner cities attend secondary schools with serious weaknesses identified by OFSTED, compared with 1 in 19 overall (Barber 1999).

A future policy strategy needs to continue efforts to link education with the wider community. General efforts to reduce social inequalities, discussed elsewhere in this report, are an important ingredient for a more equitable education system. But in addition, two particular objectives need to be pursued within education – improving the low attainment of disadvantaged groups, and reducing the concentration of disadvantage in certain schools.

Targeting low attainment and disadvantage

The education system should do everything possible to reduce present inequalities, giving all students the opportunity to succeed. In particular, this means equalising access to the same basic level of provision. Students from disadvantaged backgrounds should expect teachers, facilities and resources that are at least as good as for everybody else.

This may mean spending more money on schools and students that suffer from particular difficulties. It will also require a model of cooperation rather than competition among schools. In order to ensure that successful approaches are spread to schools serving disadvantaged groups, senior managers and teachers require appropriate training and development opportunities.

A focus on the needs of disadvantaged pupils will also require the education system to look closely at what is causing a core of students to fail. For example:

- Are different incentives for schools needed? At present the incentive for secondary schools is to concentrate help on those on the border of getting five GCSEs (near the middle of the distribution), rather than lower achievers (for whom one or two good GCSEs might make a big difference).
- Would some disadvantaged children benefit from

more alternatives to mainstream academic education, such as apprenticeships? Adequate resources are needed for such options.

Tackling concentrations of disadvantage

A persistent tension in the education system has been between the difficulties caused by social polarisation in schools and the desire of middle class families to get the best for their children. Through its Excellence in Cities policy, the Government's aim is to make disadvantaged schools better, and encourage more middle class parents to choose them. This is no easy task. The illustrations of policy shown below, and other solutions, are likely to be controversial. However, over the long term, governments need to persist in such efforts since no amount of within-school improvement is likely to work in schools with concentrations of the most disadvantaged students.

Tackling concentrations of disadvantage: Policy illustrations

- Present *'league tables'* in new ways, for example based on clusters of schools in an area, encouraging them to share resources and work together.
- Make schools with less advantaged students more attractive – for example by giving them more resources to attract the best teachers and/or permit smaller classes.
- Coordinate *admissions procedures* among groups of schools to avoid excessive social concentration in any one of them.

Conclusion: deploying resources to give priority to the disadvantaged

For too long UK spending on education as a proportion of GDP has been well below the OECD average. The Government's commitment to a major expansion in resources potentially allows everybody to benefit, but with an extra emphasis on disadvantaged groups. This could redress longstanding inequalities. It would mean devoting somewhat less than otherwise to general education improvements, but in the context of overall growth would not require cuts elsewhere.

Such a process requires better mechanisms for targeting disadvantage both within and between schools. Rigorous evaluation is needed to ensure that targeted money is well spent. Most importantly, the education system needs to raise its expectations of disadvantaged students, while providing the resources necessary to make them achievable.

Not only the young: Equal access to learning throughout life

A sound initial education for all is an essential foundation for combating disadvantage. However, it is also essential for adults to be able to continue to develop throughout their lives, adapting to changing circumstances and continuing their education and training where necessary. Yet here, too, there is damaging inequality, with those who are already the most educated and skilled being the most likely to participate (Figure 19).

The United Kingdom is relatively good at providing employer-based training to higher skilled workers. It is worse at engaging less skilled workers and those outside employment, and a bias in training opportunities towards the better educated is compounded by a bias towards those in good jobs. New avenues for less advantaged groups need therefore to focus on:

- promoting Continuous Education and Training (CET) and providing clear information and guidance for under-served groups
- subsidising work-related CET in ways that build on the experience of Individual Learning Accounts, but are more targeted on the disadvantaged – possibly by linking access to income-tested tax credits
- improving incentives to undertake training, for example through enhanced benefits.

Figure 19 **Percentage of 25- to 64-year-old employees receiving education/training, by qualification and literacy level (1994–95)**

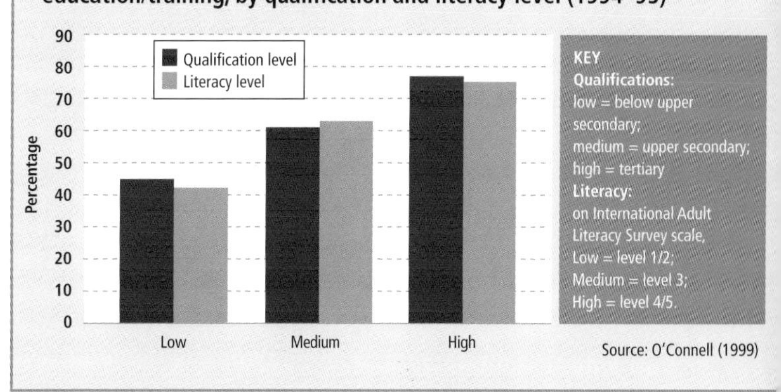

Source: O'Connell (1999)

2 Family poverty: Breaking the link with social exclusion

An integrated approach to family poverty is needed...

The alarming growth in child poverty over the past two decades has led to a historically unique political commitment to tackle the problem over the next two. At one level, this is a matter of improving the incomes of families with children, which have deteriorated in relative terms. Yet both the causes and consequences of child poverty are tied up with a range of other influences within families, ranging from low skills to poor health to limited expectations. Many children who grow up poor are being excluded from the mainstream life of a largely affluent society. An attack on income poverty needs therefore to be combined with a strategy to address other aspects of social exclusion.

Family poverty – the problem

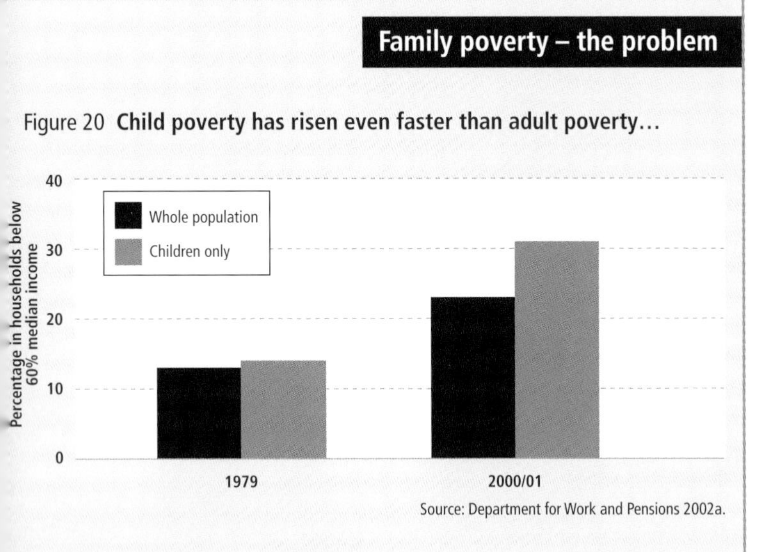

Figure 20 **Child poverty has risen even faster than adult poverty...**

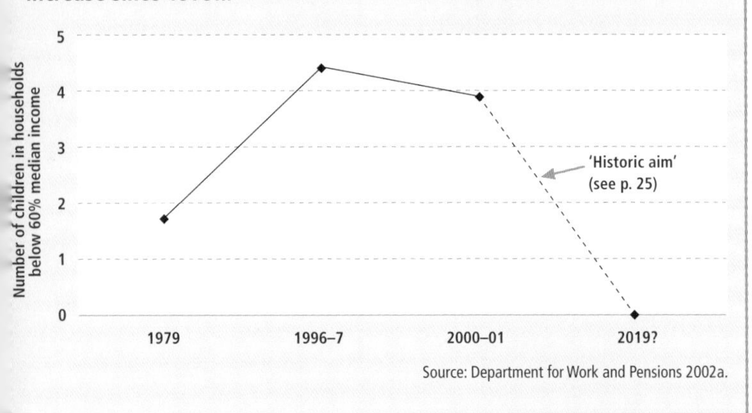

Figure 21 **...and since its peak in 1996 has fallen by only a fifth of the increase since 1979...**

... addressing child poverty, which has worsened sharply...

Between 1979 and 1996, the number of children living in households with below 60 per cent of median income more than doubled, to above 4 million. Despite a reduction in this number by half a million since 1996, 3 in 10 children remain in households with incomes below this threshold (Brewer et al. 2002).

Unlike a generation ago, poverty is now concentrated in households with children (Figure 20). The long-term rise in child poverty has thus been linked partly to general trends that have increased inequalities, such as the growing dispersion of earnings, but also to some factors that have hit families with children hardest. In particular, the number of children living in households without work has doubled since 1979, to nearly two million, of whom about half have lone parents (Dickens et al. 2001).

In the UK today, a child has more chance of living in a household with below 60 per cent median income than a child in almost any other European country, and twice as much chance as a French, Swedish or Dutch child (Bradbury and Janitti 1999).

Child poverty is a form of hardship that society finds particularly unacceptable. Joseph Rowntree Foundation research shows that parents who live in poverty often try to shield their children from its consequences, by spending less on themselves (Kempson 1996). Yet they do not fully succeed. Those in the poorest fifth of the population spend no more on their children's toys, clothes and shoes (in real terms) than they did 30 years ago (Gregg et al. 1999).

Thus the nation's poorest children have not shared in the dramatic increase in the material well-being of children generally in the UK in recent years. The Foundation's Survey of Poverty and Social Exclusion showed that two million children at the end of the twentieth century were going without items that most members of the general public considered to be necessary – because their parents could not afford them. These were things such as adequate clothing, a healthy diet and items to help their educational development (Gordon et al. 2000).

...and which passes down through the generations...

Quite apart from the direct suffering caused by the experience of child poverty, there is now strong evidence that it has a long-term detrimental effect on people's lives, and therefore often repeats itself from one generation to the next. JRF research has shown that even when they are in their 30s, adults have less chance of working and more chance of low pay if their families faced financial hardship when they were growing up (Figures 22 and 23). This poverty effect is over and above the effect of associated phenomena such as unemployment. Poverty is also a key element in the disadvantage faced by many children growing up in lone parent families; those who are not poor face similar chances in adulthood whether they grew up with two parents or one.

...but poverty must also be seen in the context of a range of related family difficulties.
The recurrence of disadvantage that can occur from one generation to the next involves a range of factors associated with poverty, including poor health, low qualifications, antisocial behaviour and, for a minority, the experience of growing up in care. The link between low income and wider disadvantage across generations is illustrated by the finding that parents who experienced poverty as children are more likely to have children who perform poorly at school. Any solutions need therefore to address a range of risk factors that make young people potentially vulnerable throughout childhood. These range from individual characteristics such as behavioural disorders and health, to family circumstances, to the level of support they receive from their local communities.

The Government's war on child poverty has made a promising start, but has reached only the end of the beginning
The present government has acknowledged the unacceptability of child poverty in a prosperous society. In March 1999, the Prime Minister stated:

> *"Our historic aim will be for ours to be the first generation to end child poverty...It is a 20 year mission."*

In the past five years, a start has been made through a combination of three kinds of policy:

Redistribution of income towards families with children, through a two-track policy that gives something to all such families, but more to the poor. Budgets from 1998 onwards have consistently redistributed to poorer groups and to children. The Child Tax Credit will from March 2003 give the Government a single instrument for directing money to children according to their means, regardless of other aspects of family circumstances. Much (although by no means all) of this help goes to families with below 60 per cent median income.

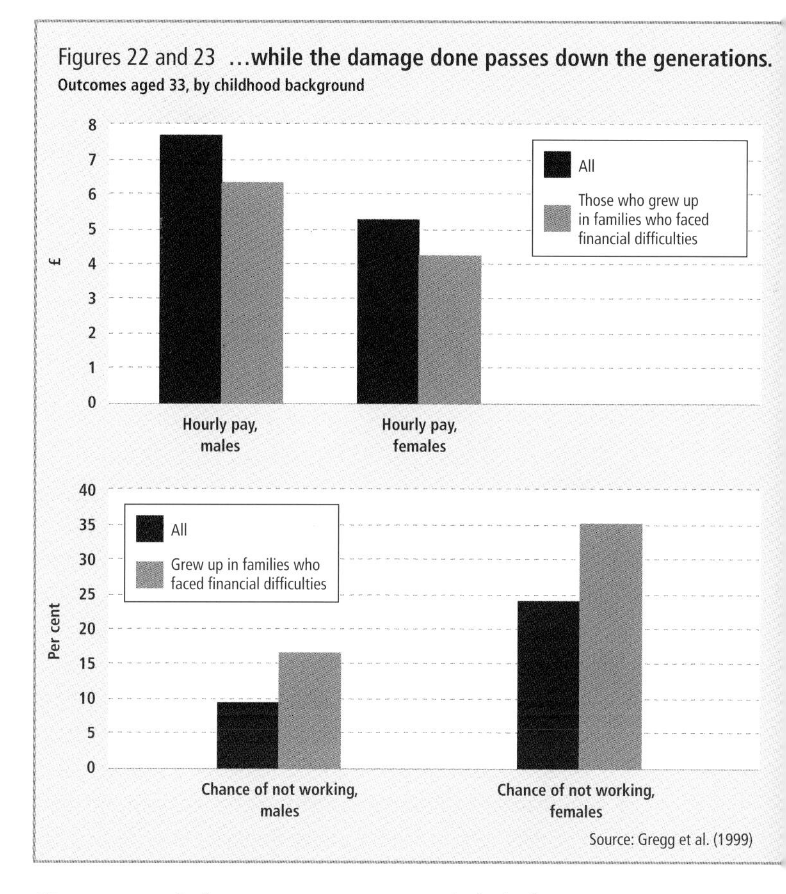

Measures to help parents to enter work, including the New Deal for Lone Parents, tax credits for childcare and a greater number of childcare places.

Initiatives to tackle wider social exclusion, including in particular the Sure Start programme of comprehensive support services to families with young children in disadvantaged neighbourhoods, and the Children's Fund offering support for older children and their parents.

Efforts to reduce poverty have made some early progress, with a slow but steady fall in the number of children with no parent working, and an apparent (modest) reversal of the rise in the number of children in families with low incomes (Figure 21). However, this is only the start of a very long journey, for two important reasons.

First, even if conditions were to stay the same, it gets relatively harder to lift people out of poverty, since the first beneficiaries have been primarily those close to the threshold, such as low-income working families, rather than those in deeper poverty.

Second, it is harder because in practice, conditions will not stay the same. Some factors, such as widening wage differences, could make the task harder. Others, such as economic downturns, will test political resolve. To complete the mission, courage and determination will be needed.

Tackling family poverty: A broad-based strategy

The first principle stated in Part I is to help people achieve their potential. For children, this means not just offering educational opportunities but also enabling them to grow up free of poverty and disadvantage, which prevent them from taking full advantage of these opportunities.

Of all the policy areas reviewed in this report, child poverty is the one where a commitment to tackle disadvantage is at present the strongest in government strategy. Yet the problems that remain are deeply entrenched and require long-term solution. This is partly a matter of committing sufficient resources to enable children to escape income poverty, but must also include a wide range of other measures to help families whose problems are not wholly financial.

Sustaining the assault on child poverty

Few would disagree with Gordon Brown, the Chancellor of the Exchequer, that child poverty is a "scar on the nation's soul". But it seems increasingly unlikely that his commitment to halve child poverty by 2010 and then eradicate it "within a generation" can be met unless the goal is pursued with still greater vigour. The modest progress made so far despite some bold measures demonstrates the magnitude of the task.

With the launch of a new system to support families with children in 2003, the structures are in place to sustain this assault. What will matter is maintaining a commitment to allocate sufficient resources to such support, which may require tough decisions about taxation and other spending priorities.

Services delivering support to families

Public policy has to strike a balance between providing legitimate support for families in their role of raising healthy, competent and confident children, and avoiding excessive intervention in the private sphere of people's lives. The important thing is for governments to support families without either stigmatising them or trying to substitute for parents, other than in extreme circumstances where children's safety is at risk.

Two promising current examples of hands-on support for families in disadvantaged communities are Sure Start and the Children's Fund, providing positive help for parents of children under 4 and aged 5 to 13 respectively. They work because they bring together a range of different services to provide comprehensive support that involves families in managing their own development.

Long-term policy goals

- Sustain the assault on child poverty.
- Structure services to offer direct help to parents and children in dealing with their lives, where it is needed.
- Extend family support in new directions where needed, for example to help support relationships and work–life balance.

In order to extend and sustain these efforts, which so far cater for only a minority of children in poor households, the approach of these support services needs to be integrated into 'mainstream' services. The commitment in the 2002 Comprehensive Spending Review to pilot Children's Trusts which integrate all children's services is a radical step in this direction. A further welcome step would be to stop measuring the success of services in terms of 'service outputs' – the volume of services delivered to families – and instead develop services according to how well they improve children's lives ('outcome-based' planning). This would encourage a pooling of resources among agencies, and the involvement of children and parents, in efforts to achieve the desired results.

Tackling child poverty: policy illustrations

- Adopt a budget rule that increases in the income that supports children in the worst-off families should *consistently be equal to or exceed the general rise in living standards*. For the first time, the Child Tax Credit gives a simple mechanism to pursue this goal in relation to all poor families, in and out of work.
- Over a sustained period prioritise the income of *non-working families with children*, whose income mainly remains well below the 60 per cent of median income target. Specifically, aim to ensure that the overall income of these families – which include an 'adult' as well as a 'child' portion – rises relative to median incomes.
- Look closely at and address the causes of lack of take-up of present entitlements. About 1 1/2 million children live in households with below 60 per cent of median who are not receiving either Income Support or tax credits (Brewer et al. 2002).

Extending family support in new directions
As well as reforming the overall structure of services to families, the scope of family support needs to be reconsidered in the years ahead. What new kinds of action are needed to address changing demographic and social trends? Three areas actively considered by the Joseph Rowntree Foundation concern early parenthood, relationship support and work–life balance.

Early parenthood Britain has the highest teenage birth rate in Western Europe (despite a modest fall in recent years). Young mothers are more likely than average to come from disadvantaged families, and their children are more likely to be raised in poverty. With a general trend among most couples to start families later, Britain risks a growing polarisation between double-income families with older parents, and those who have become parents early, especially those mothers not living with their child's father at the time of birth or during early childhood.

Research findings show the importance of a range of support services addressed to this latter group. They start with the importance of school education, which can be at least as likely to discourage early pregnancy as contraception advice. Advice after conception together with pre- and post-natal support are also critical. Support focused on early pregnancy and parenthood should not be confined literally to 'teen pregnancy', since the evidence shows that risks of poverty and exclusion are also disproportionately high for people who become parents in their early 20s (Figure 24).

Relationship support Ministers have maintained that Government should have no part in cajoling people into marriage, nor in compelling them to remain together when relationships break down. However, more public resources devoted to supporting parental relationships can benefit children, since research demonstrates the long-term damage to their well-being and prospects where ties with either parent are broken.

Research also shows, more directly, that adverse economic and environmental factors, including low income and poor housing, can harm children through the stress placed on parents. As well as combating these factors, more can be done to help parents experiencing them.

A more sensitive matter is the status of parents in couples, whether cohabiting or married. Stronger, more committed relationships tend to lead to marriage, yet in Britain more relationships break down both among cohabiting parents and among those who marry after the birth of a child than in other European countries. France has introduced 'Civil Solidarity Pacts' for parents who do not wish to marry, many of whom welcome the rights, responsibilities and recognition that such pacts confer on a relationship. This option merits further investigation for the UK.

Work–life balance Low-income parents, especially lone parents, can face tough choices about whether to support their children by earning income or by staying at home with them. Decisions are influenced by the choices on offer, most notably access to high quality childcare. While much emphasis has so far been placed on moving from welfare to work, policies that allow parents to spend more time supporting their children may in the long term be just as important to reducing social exclusion. There is some evidence that the support that parents can give at home, especially to pre-school children, can make a substantial difference to their future development.

Thus, rather than promoting either going out to work or staying at home, governments and employers need to improve the quality of options and provide real choice. This means both further improvements to childcare and rules to ensure better choices at work – rules that remain weaker in the UK than in many other European countries.

Figure 24 **Early motherhood and adult social exclusion: the proportion of women experiencing given outcomes by age at birth of first baby**

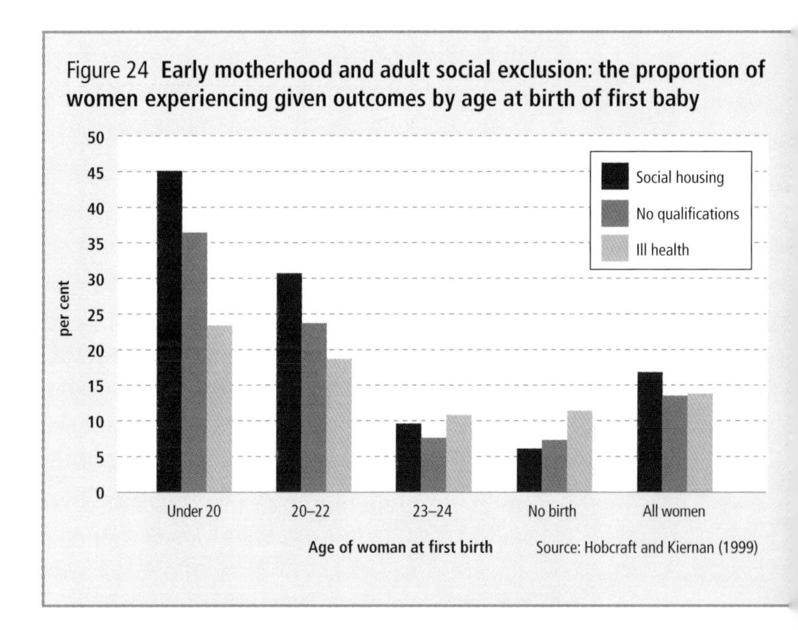

Work–life balance: Policy illustrations

- Measures to allow *changes in hours* for family reasons, through tougher conditions on employers.
- More rigorous enforcement of the EU *Working Time Directive*.
- Measures to ensure that *employees are properly informed* of family friendly options.

3 Unequal places: Disadvantage and geographic difference

Policies to help disadvantaged places have focused on the local…

The distribution of disadvantage in the UK today has a strongly geographic dimension. A world of difference separates the poorest neighbourhoods where jobs are scarce and where poverty and associated social problems are the norm, from booming areas where the greatest difficulty is the shortage of staff for domestic and public services.

Recognising these stark contrasts, the government has launched regeneration policies which focus on the most deprived neighbourhoods and local authorities. At the same time, regional bodies are being given an enhanced role, particularly in relation to economic development, with the establishment of Regional Development Agencies. However, the focus of the new regional approach, especially in England, has not been to address poverty and disadvantage.

The Joseph Rowntree Foundation's research has shown the importance of locally based regeneration. The following analysis does not seek to diminish the significance of neighbourhood renewal efforts, but focuses on the regional dimension, which has received less attention.

…but regional differences, especially between the south and north, cannot be ignored…

Although there are great variations within regions, differences in the prosperity and the concentration of disadvantage across different regions of the country are considerable. And they matter.

The United Kingdom today has regions well below and well above the EU average, in terms of income per head (Figure 25). While there are pockets of poverty in all regions, the chance of being poor varies widely by region. The 10 per cent of local authorities with the worst concentrations of disadvantage are primarily in the north, with none in the south outside London (Figure 26).

There are three particular reasons to pay attention to these regional differences:

The mismatch in housing demand and supply This creates contrasting frictions. In the south-east, the housing supply crisis obliges many to live in overcrowded or temporary homes and is causing a key worker shortage. In the north, low housing demand is threatening the viability of services where population densities fall and at worst has led to a virtual abandoning of some neighbourhoods.

Large clusters of deprived areas In some parts of the north, these clusters are making escape more difficult, creating stigma and limiting their residents' opportunities.

The effect of economic restructuring The factors that have driven a widening of these disparities have yet to run their course. As economic restruturing continues, strong regions are able to build on their comparative advantage, and weaker ones suffer (Cambridge Econometrics 2002). Without significant policy intervention, regional differences risk increasing in the next 20 years.

…with employment differences especially significant…

The critical difference between better- and worse-off regions is the development of job opportunities. London had 16 per cent more jobs in 2001 than in 1995; in the north of England and Scotland there was no growth overall, and a fall in full-time male employment (Cambridge Econometrics 2002).

In deprived areas of the south, in particular within London, there is great potential to help disadvantaged groups improve their ability to access jobs. In regions where jobs are generally scarce, this is harder. In these areas the New Deal has a poorer record in finding people jobs. Where it has found jobs, they are more likely in these regions to be short-lived or of lower quality (Sunley et al. 2001).

…and continuously compounded by the location of markets and skills.

Regional employment differences originate largely from the decline in manufacturing in formerly industrial regions, and the natural advantages of London and the south as service industry centres. These differences are being compounded over time by virtuous and vicious circles. Firms want to locate employment where there are plentiful skills and prosperous local markets. Since some of these markets and skills come from the presence of other successful companies, there is a tendency for successful services industries to cluster. Companies benefit from informal networking among specialists in the same industry, and from an area's prosperity, which creates markets for a range of services such as leisure and retail.

At a regional level, there is constant interaction between the kinds of job available and the competence of the workforce. While all regions have just over a third of people working in middle-level jobs, in London there are twice as many in professional, managerial and technical occupations than in the least skilled work, whereas in the former industrial regions there are similar numbers in both categories (National Statistics 2002). As these different profiles attract different kinds of jobs, some regions could become increasingly dominated by low-skill, low-paid employment from which it is hard to escape.

More specifically, three key factors feeding into high productivity are unevenly distributed through the regions:

Skills In London, the south-east and the east of England, a much larger proportion of young people stay in full-time education than in most regions (Department for Education and Skills 2002), and this is compounded by a 'brain drain' of graduates moving to these regions from others.

Investment and innovation London and the south-east are better placed to attract new private investment whether from Britain or overseas. Despite high profile cases of inward investment in depressed regions, it is the favoured ones that attract the most. However, public sector investment cannot be ignored, and in more depressed areas plays a major role in the local economy.

Enterprise and competition Nineteen out of the 20 local authorities with the highest rates of business formation are in the south. Even in periods of economic growth, some less favoured regions have seen more businesses closing than starting up. This shortfall feeds the underlying disadvantages of the region by failing to create a competitive business environment with a drive for increased productivity, research and development and workforce training (HM Treasury/Department of Trade and Industry 2001).

Geography – the problem

Figure 25 **UK regions vary in wealth from well above to well below the EU average...**

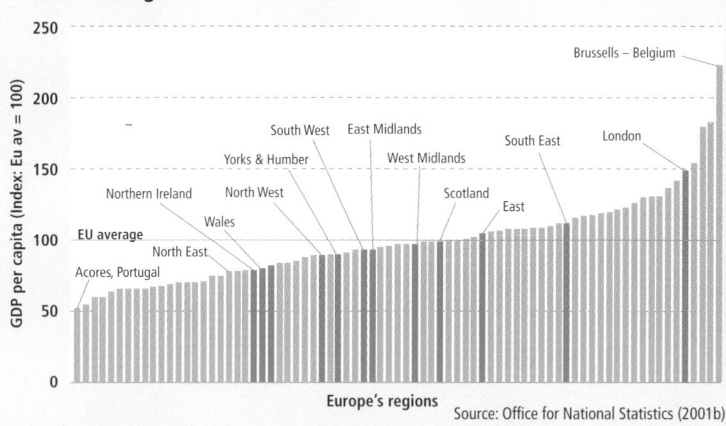

Figure 26 **...with up to a half of people in some regions living in the country's most deprived local authorities in England...**

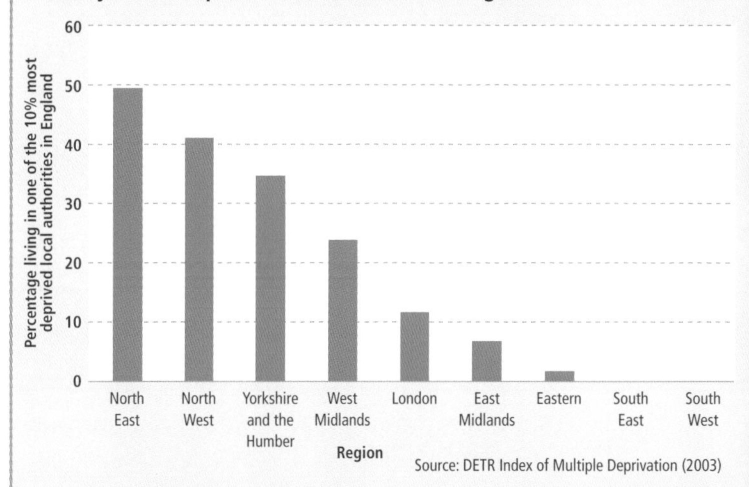

Figure 27 **...and differences accentuated by variations in the occupational profiles of different regions.**

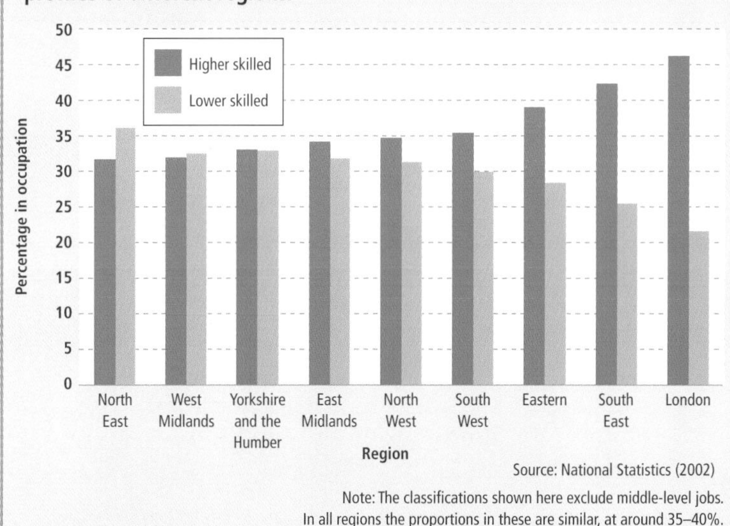

Note: The classifications shown here exclude middle-level jobs. In all regions the proportions in these are similar, at around 35–40%.

Tackling geographic disadvantage: Developing the regions

Contrary to common belief, the growth of different regions in the United Kingdom is not a zero-sum game. If depressed regions can attract more investment and generate more prosperity, this need not come at the expense of presently successful ones, and indeed can help them. It can help take pressure off an overheated housing market in the south, while creating a more balanced and sustainable level of prosperity in the nation as a whole.

For individuals and for local communities, a healthy regional economy is an important background factor: it is much harder for those suffering disadvantage to realise their potential if they live in a depressed area of the country.

Supporting private investment

Traditionally, regional development has been closely concerned with the use of fiscal measures to help attract private investment to disadvantaged regions. Government has a variety of tools for doing so, including preferential tax rates, capital allowances, government grants and subsidies.

The research evidence shows that such measures can have significant benefits. Regions in Europe that have succeeded in lifting their economic performance have all benefited from serious investment from national or European funds. Yet annual spending on the UK's most important tool, Regional Selective Assistance, has declined steadily, and such support is only around a third of the EU average (see Figure 28). There is a strong case for reversing this trend.

Inward investment and locally generated growth cannot be seen as alternatives, but as complementary routes to regional revival.

Long-term policy goals

- Complement measures to encourage local growth with active support for outside investment in deprived regions.
- Deploy public spending in ways that help regions grow.
- Ensure adequate investment in the 'hard' (physical) and 'soft' (people/networks) infrastructure needed for an 'urban renaissance'.
- Help rural communities to develop the capacity to support geographically dispersed disadvantaged groups.
- Encourage a civic culture that enables communities to design solutions to their own difficulties.

Deploying public spending

Direct public spending on mainstream government programmes will always be far higher than any government support for private regional investment. Can such public spending be targeted to help disadvantaged regions? Much of this spending – for example on schools and hospitals – needs to be spent throughout the country, and even measures privileging disadvantaged clients advocated elsewhere in this report would not have a big regional effect. A number of spending decisions may take into account regional development factors; some illustrative examples are listed opposite. In such decisions, regional economic development could become an explicit factor, while not the only one that determines the outcome.

One lesson from the past, however, is that public employment is never itself enough to revive an area: such investment is best employed as part of a wider strategy in which conditions for private investment are also created, so that the stimulus from public jobs can be fully exploited.

Encouraging an urban renaissance

The revival of depressed regions outside the south of England will require a turnaround in the fortunes of these regions' big cities. The Urban Taskforce and Urban White Paper have envisaged economic revival for Britain's towns and cities, drawing more on the experience of European cities like Barcelona and Amsterdam than on British precedent.

Some cities appear to have begun to turn the corner with people and jobs returning. However, important pockets of poverty remain, and the success of cities such as Leeds has not so far spread outwards to neighbouring places such as Bradford. A strategy aiming to push this revival further will need to:

- Help spread success rather than assume a trickle out effect. This requires the building of linkages around subregional centres, whether physical transport links or in terms of governance – for example co-ordinating the approaches of planning authorities.
- Avoid polarisation within cities, as has occurred in London, by aiming to develop mixed income and mixed age communities and by helping the least skilled and educated to acquire training and education that will allow them to access new jobs.
- Address the problems of areas with low housing demand, which has a knock-on effect on the attractiveness and viability of parts of large cities.

Deploying public spending to regions: Policy illustrations

- Consider regional factors when awarding government contracts – ranging from major defence procurement to small one-off contracts.
- Site major government investment strategically, for example in new higher education facilities.
- Site civil service offices (for either new or relocated functions) strategically.

Such policies have a promising precedent in the public sector relocation out of London that followed the Flemming Report in 1963. Although the primary driver was to save public money, the policy helped create good quality and skilled employment not vulnerable to the economic cycle, and had positive multiplier effects generating private sector activity (Jefferson and Trainor 1996).

Economic regeneration will not create an urban renaissance if inner city neighbourhoods are so unattractive that people commute to the new jobs from outside. Such problems can be addressed partly through better management of the social housing sector but in some areas such as Manchester and Liverpool, large-scale renewal of the physical and social infrastructure will be needed. In these areas, new vehicles such as regeneration companies need to be capable of bringing public and private resources to bear on an entire sub-regional housing market.

Tackling exclusion in rural areas

Poverty and disadvantage are not confined to the urban areas of Britain. In rural areas, social exclusion is widespread, though often hidden (Joseph Rowntree Foundation 2000). The risk here is that growing general affluence makes life harder for those without resources, for example through limited transport and housing options. Here, concentrated area-based initiatives are less appropriate than in cities, but the need for amenities such as social housing is strong. To involve those affected in local initiatives, new approaches to capacity-building are therefore required, adapted to the rural situation where problems are less geographically concentrated.

Encouraging bottom-up solutions

Within and between regions, local diversity demands a variety of responses to the problem of regeneration. Decentralisation of decision making is needed, not merely in order to deliver central priorities more efficiently but to help shape the agenda.

Figure 28 **Spending per head on regional aid by EU member states**

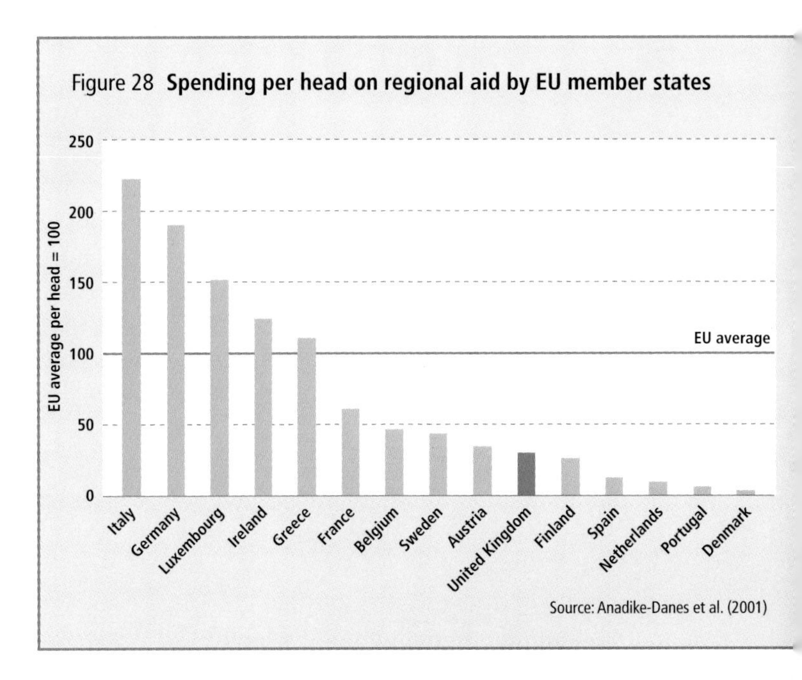

Source: Anadike-Danes et al. (2001)

A key challenge for government in the years ahead will be to ensure that such efforts are more than just a panoply of disjointed initiatives. In particular, policies at national, regional and local levels need to be integrated, ensuring that they are complementary and that individual policies in each case are implemented at the most appropriate spatial level.

Local solutions: Policy illustration

Support 'catalyst' projects, such as festivals, and the 'recovery' of local public spaces, with strong involvement from the local community. Major events such as the Commonwealth Games in Manchester may also be important in building social capital by enhancing local pride and identity.

4 Supporting incomes for vulnerable groups

This report has pointed to a damaging rise in the number of people on a low income…

The number of people in households with less than 60 per cent of median income has more than doubled over the past 20 years. This report has called for a concerted effort over the next 20 years to minimise the number with incomes below that threshold. It does so first because so many households are failing to attain what is agreed to be a basic living standard in the twenty-first century, and second on the basis that a prosperous country can afford to allocate some of its future growth to gradually improving the relative position of the worst off.

…during a period when the impact of economic and demographic trends have been compounded by benefit stringency…

The growth in inequalities has been influenced by a range of long-term social and economic trends, summarised on pages 10–11. These have resulted in particular in a growth in the number of households that have members of working age, but with nobody in work. With the number of pensioners also rising over the long term, the number of people depending on benefits to keep them out of poverty has increased.

However, the actual poverty rate is influenced not just by the number on benefits but by the relative incomes of people in particular situations, whether in low-paid work or depending on particular benefits. For those in work, relative pay has fallen steadily (see Figure 5, page 10). For those not working, income depends on the adequacy of various benefits.

Supporting income – the problem

Figure 29 **With benefits stagnant in real terms, they have steadily fallen as a percentage of average earnings**

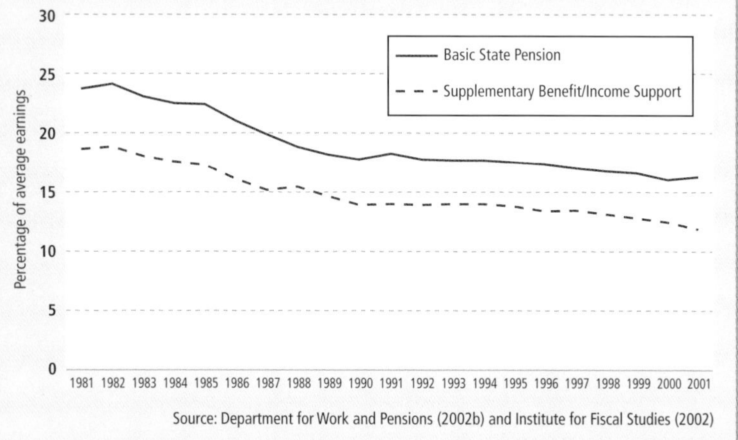

Source: Department for Work and Pensions (2002b) and Institute for Fiscal Studies (2002)

In practice, Governments keen to contain a mounting welfare bill have contributed to the relative decline of the incomes of the poorest by generally uprating benefits only in line with prices rather than rising earnings over most of the past two decades (Figure 29).

The present government has gone some way towards reversing this policy, for selected groups. In particular, there have been sharp rises in benefits for children, and in means-tested benefits for pensioners. However, with these exceptions, benefits have continued to rise more slowly than general living standards, and some key benefits such as the state retirement pension remain well below their former value relative to earnings (Department for Work and Pensions 2002a). Most importantly for the long term, there has been no general commitment to restore a link between rises in benefits and rises in earnings. In such circumstances, there is a risk that the value of benefits will continue to erode over the long term: in hard times, governments find it hard to afford to increase them in real terms, while in high-growth periods even generous increases may fail to raise their value relative to earnings, which are also rapidly rising.

…and dependence on means-tested support has grown.

In the postwar welfare state, there was an idea that full employment would provide adequate incomes for most people of working age, with insurance benefits covering contingencies like unemployment and sickness, as well as a basic income in retirement. Today, benefits for contingencies such as unemployment and retirement have fallen in relative value, as have earnings at the bottom end of the labour market.

To compensate, the government has broadened the role of means-tested benefits and tax credits. Most unemployed people depend on such benefits. Pensioner incomes are being maintained relative to earnings not through the retirement pension but through a Minimum Income Guarantee, and soon through a Pensioner Credit that will top up incomes for half of all pensioners. For those in work, top-ups for low incomes have been increased in the present tax credit regime, and from 2003 will be extended beyond the present target groups (families with children and disabled people).

A guarantee that nobody's income will fall below a particular level is an essential part in any strategy for tackling disadvantage. However, such guarantees work better if they are a back-up to other measures. If means-testing becomes the mainstay of a system to tackle income disadvantage, a number of risks arise.

Means-testing may reduce people's incentives to provide for themselves. The government is keen to avoid this, and has ensured through tax credits that people who take work and those who have saved for their pensions are better off as a result. However, in order to do so, it has had to extend means testing to a much larger number of people on low to middle incomes. They face high effective marginal tax rates, as benefits are withdrawn with rising income. Too much means-tested support of in-work incomes therefore risks undermining, over the long term, the incentive of households to take steps to enhance their own earnings – whether by improving their skills or by increasing their working hours (for example through a second person in the household working).

Such withdrawal effects create new poverty traps, and may be seen as unfair, even if they do not determine behaviour. They limit the capacity of households to raise their net incomes above a certain just-adequate level.

Take-up of means-tested benefits is often relatively low, partly because of stigma attached to claiming. This means that in practice they do not ensure minimum incomes for all. The government is trying to reduce stigma, but take-up rates remain an issue. For example, 38 per cent of those entitled are estimated not to claim Working Families Tax Credit[6] and between 22 per cent and 36 per cent do not take up the Minimum Income Guarantee. This contrasts with near-universal take up of non-means tested benefits such as Child Benefit and the State Retirement Pension.

Tackling income: Routes out of poverty

A strategy to ensure that, 20 years from now, as few people as possible live on incomes below 60 per cent of median needs to operate on several fronts simultaneously. In particular, such a strategy must apply the first principle for tackling disadvantage proposed in Part I, of helping people achieve their potential, in combination with the second, of creating an adequate income floor.

Enhancing earnings from paid work

The greatest potential to improve people's incomes remains with paid work. For people who are not working and want to, a focus by government on assistance in moving into jobs has been a helpful strategy.

However, somewhat less attention has been given to the task of enabling people to thrive in the working world, in terms of getting stable, high quality jobs that are well enough paid to avoid having to fall back on means-tested support in order to obtain an adequate income. Even though some working families with high levels of need may always require some extra assistance even if wages rise, a sustainable long-term reduction in poverty rates would be helped greatly by improved earning power among the lowest paid. This would help to sustain them in their working years and also improve their ability to save for retirement.

Is it possible to start reversing a long-standing trend towards more unequal rewards in the labour market? Wage and income dispersion in OECD countries appears to be closely associated with education and skill inequalities (Figure 30). Thus any strategy to reduce low pay must centre around the twin objectives of improving 'human capital' and raising productivity.

Figure 30 **The UK's relatively unequal earnings distribution is associated with its unequal skill distribution**

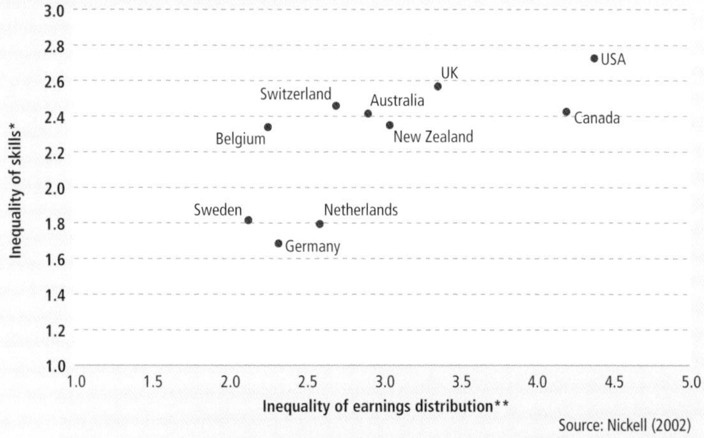

Inequality of skills* (vertical axis, 1.0–3.0); Inequality of earnings distribution** (horizontal axis, 1.0–5.0)

USA, UK, Canada, Switzerland, Australia, New Zealand, Belgium, Sweden, Netherlands, Germany

Source: Nickell (2002)

Notes: * Ratio of 95th percentile to 5th percentile score in adult literacy test (OECD 1996)
** Ratio of 90th to 10th percentile earnings (OECD 1997)

Better education and training, discussed on pages 20–23, are central. However, they are not enough. Government and employers also need to work together to ensure that the right skills are developed and that they are used productively at the workplace. This mission goes hand in hand with encouraging employers to invest more in training their less qualified workers.

Long-term policy goals

- Enhance earnings from work.
- Create a sound basis for providing incomes to needy groups outside the labour market, meeting the principle of minimising the number of people below 60 per cent of the median.
- Give greater recognition to those who undertake socially valued activities outside paid work.

At the same time as improving skills and productivity, it should be possible to raise the earnings floor progressively through upratings in the minimum wage. As a start, governments interested in raising low wages will want to increase the minimum to the greatest extent possible without threatening jobs. But while pay increases cannot sustainably run ahead of productivity increases, one aim can be to raise them in tandem. Over a sustained period, the knowledge by employers that the minimum wage will be increased annually, at least in proportion to average earnings and where possible faster, will create an incentive to think of ways of improving productivity.

If such a strategy succeeds, tax credits to top up low working incomes would not disappear but could be expected to play a more incidental role. The government has already created a separate mechanism, the Child Tax Credit, to recognise the extra needs of families with children – this is no longer specifically a support for work, but a wider form of support for people inside and outside work on lower incomes. The credit more specifically designed to make work pay, the Working Tax Credit, might eventually be reduced to the role of a temporary safety net and a bridge into work rather than a long-term income top-up for people stuck on low pay.

Provision for needy groups outside the labour market

A large number of people of working age, and the great majority of older people, have to live for lengthy periods without income from work. The 'insurance' principle for providing income during these periods in return for contribution during working periods has more or less

More stable non-work incomes: Policy illustrations

- For people with disabilities that limit their capacity for work, a single stable payment similar to the Child Tax Credit would allow greater flexibility. This could be paid whether the person was not working or was in low-paid/erratic employment, and would only be withdrawn for people who find good stable jobs. It would be separate from the allowance paid to severely disabled people, regardless of means, to help them cope with their disabilities.
- Retired people with limited means would benefit from stronger entitlements that would reduce the need for means-testing. Possibilities include:
  - speeding up the introduction of a second state pension to guarantee something like 60 per cent of median income, which at present could take 50 years
  - raising the value of the main state pension to the level of the minimum income guarantee, and peg it to earnings[8]
  - introducing a further tier of pensions supported by compulsory insurance
  - a new state retirement pension at two levels, with the present minimum income guarantee level for people on modest incomes and a lower level, equal to the present retirement pension, for the better off.

broken down in the UK, with means-tested benefits now being the principal guarantee.

Attitude surveys show considerable public support for giving more generous benefits to certain groups who have good reasons not to work, or to work less than other groups – notably parents, disabled people and retired people.

A strategy for systematically supporting their incomes could usefully be guided by two objectives. The first is to provide out-of-work incomes that rise systematically with increasing prosperity. The second is to avoid making excessive use of means tests, and to balance income-dependent benefit with a stable structure of broad entitlements. A means-tested safety net will have to play some role in moving towards a guarantee of 60 per cent median income, but it should not be the sole measure.

Recent changes in the way in which families with children are being supported illustrates how both of these goals can be pursued. After many years in which some children's benefits (and especially Child Benefit) have declined in relative terms, support for children has been sharply increased and at least partially pegged to rises in earnings.[7] The reformed benefits and tax credits system being completed in 2003 offers a combination of some support for everyone and extra support for those on low incomes. For poorer families, there is not a narrow means test, but rather a flat rate of Child Tax Credit that gives all families earning below a certain level a flat rate payment, whether or not they are working.

Other groups facing long-term uncertainties over their incomes could also benefit from stronger guarantees of this kind. People whose disabilities prevent them from getting stable employment find it hard to cope with the present system, especially if they move in and out of work. People with limited means are among those facing growing uncertainty about whether they will have an adequate income in retirement. They need a stronger bedrock of guaranteed support. It is not in the scope of this report to redesign the social security system, but the box on the left illustrates the kind of policy that potentially could pursue this goal.

Valuing activities outside paid work

The present government's mantra is 'work for those who can, security for those who cannot'. Yet it is not helpful to regard people outside paid work as helpless beings whose only need is support. An alternative is to encourage a range of activities – such as learning, caring and volunteering – that add social value.

As a minimum it is important not to create conditions that deter participation in activities outside work for fear of losing entitlement to benefit. A more ambitious aim would be to create extra rewards for particularly valued activities.

Rewarding valued activities: Policy illustration

- A more generous and flexible carers' allowance could be combined with an exemption of income received for personal caring (whether from public or private sources) from tests that determine benefit and tax credit entitlements. Such measures would acknowledge that society benefits from a large amount of free informal care. With the number of children forecast to decline while the number of older people rises, the relative importance of encouraging family- and community-based support for older generations will grow.

5 Housing: The twin crises of supply and affordability

Housing shortages affect everyone, but disadvantaged people the most.

In Britain today, homes are being built at much too slow a rate to match growth in demand. This is resulting in shortages in some areas of the country, which could get very much worse in the next 20 years.

The consequences of these shortages are many and varied. Everyone in areas of the country where housing is scarce is likely to be affected in some way, whether through limited housing opportunities, higher mortgages, long commutes or a deterioration of certain public services that are having difficulty recruiting and retaining staff.

The most severe effects, however, are felt by the least affluent families, unable to buy or rent satisfactory housing. At worst, they are driven into temporary accommodation or become homeless. Fewer people are now being accepted by local authorities as homeless, but a shortage of social housing has meant that most of these – and twice as many as in the 1990s – are having to live in temporary accommodation rather than being rehoused (Wilcox 2001).

They arise partly from underlying economic and demographic trends…

The demand for new housing is being driven by changes in the way in which an affluent Britain chooses to live, and related to this, how many households are being formed:

- With rising living standards, people want to live very differently than they did a century ago – in smaller households each occupying a self-contained house or flat, rather than in large extended families.
- As people live longer, they are spending more time occupying homes that are often large relative to the number of people living in the household.
- Single-person households are increasing (Figure 32), not just because there are more older people but also because people of working age are forming couples at later ages, and many divorce or separate (Office for National Statistics 2001a).
- Net migration from other countries is forecast to grow nearly 50 per cent faster than was being predicted as recently as 1998 (GAD 2002).

These trends are not all bad news in themselves: it is good that people are living longer and meeting new aspirations. The problem is for housing policies to keep up with them without creating hardship that arises from shortages.

…creating over 4 million extra households between 2001 and 2021…

Taking these factors together, it is not easy to produce accurate forecasts of growth in household numbers. Recent analysis by the Joseph Rowntree Foundation suggests that earlier official forecasts overestimated the ratio of households to population. However this is

Housing – the problem

Figure 31 **Housebuilding is at its lowest long-term rate since the 1920s…**

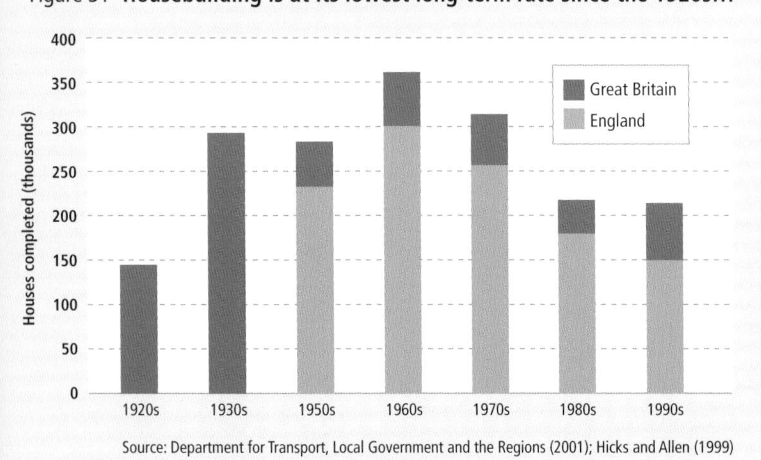

Source: Department for Transport, Local Government and the Regions (2001); Hicks and Allen (1999)

Figure 32 **…which coincides with growing demand, from factors such as the increase in single households…**

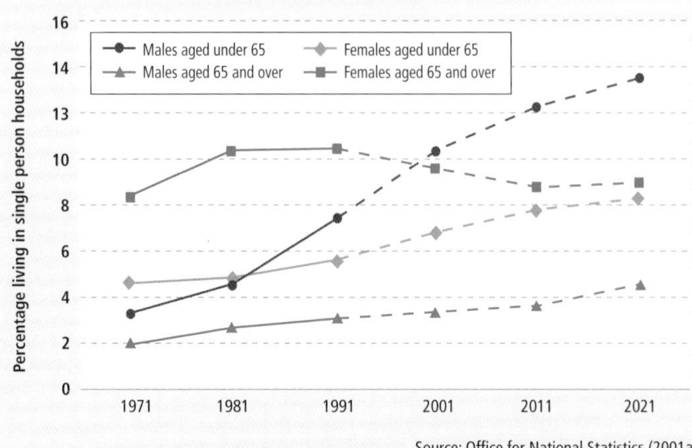

Source: Office for National Statistics (2001a)

partly offset by the higher number of expected immigrants.

The Foundation now estimates that 210,000 new homes a year will be needed in England over the next 20 years. While this is 7–11 per cent below the previous official estimate, it is far above recent building rates. These are at a historic low (Figure 31) and are falling, with less than 130,000 completed homes in England in 2001 (Wilcox 2002). The result, on present, trends would be a shocking shortfall of over a million homes in 20 years' time.[9]

...but are exacerbated by uneven demand...

These overall trends mask completely different situations in various parts of the country. In parts of major conurbations, demand remains low, and is already exceeded by supply. Here, the challenge is to improve existing conditions to help reverse decline, or in some cases to 'manage decline' by clearing estates and streets in neighbourhoods whose demise seems irreversible.

In contrast, in much of southern England, demand for housing already outstrips supply. In the years ahead, the south will bear the brunt of the pressure from increasing household numbers. Contrary to popular belief, this is not caused primarily by people moving south to find jobs. Of the population growth in the south outside London in the 1990s:

- half came from outward migration from London
- one-quarter was from natural population growth
- just under a fifth came from (net) international migration
- only one-twelfth came from (net) inter-regional migration.

London is a special case. Here, outward migration is more than balanced by high international immigration and high natural population growth. Immigrants include the extremes of rich and poor, but growing pressure on housing risks creating particular difficulties for the latter, in the absence of sufficient social housing (Bate et al. 2000).

...and by problems in supply.

Why is the housing market failing to create a sufficient supply of new homes to meet demand? This case of market failure can be linked to three factors in particular – construction industry problems, limits to land supply and lack of affordability.

Construction industry problems These include skill and labour shortages, and various process/system failings highlighted by the Latham and Egan reports (Latham 1994; Egan 1998). Some of these difficulties could be addressed in the years ahead, for example by better procurement procedures, more efficient, factory-based building techniques and improved training.

Limits to land supply Land supply is constrained largely by the planning system. The difficulty in obtaining permission to build on any previously undeveloped ('greenfield') land has grown with the combination of local opposition from the already well-housed and a strengthening of campaigns to prevent development for wider environmental reasons. Permission is easier on recycled ('brownfield') development land, but housebuilders often find it less attractive because of higher cost and the likelihood of lower demand.

Figure 33 **...with the poor suffering most because of a sharp decline in the number of social housing properties being built.**

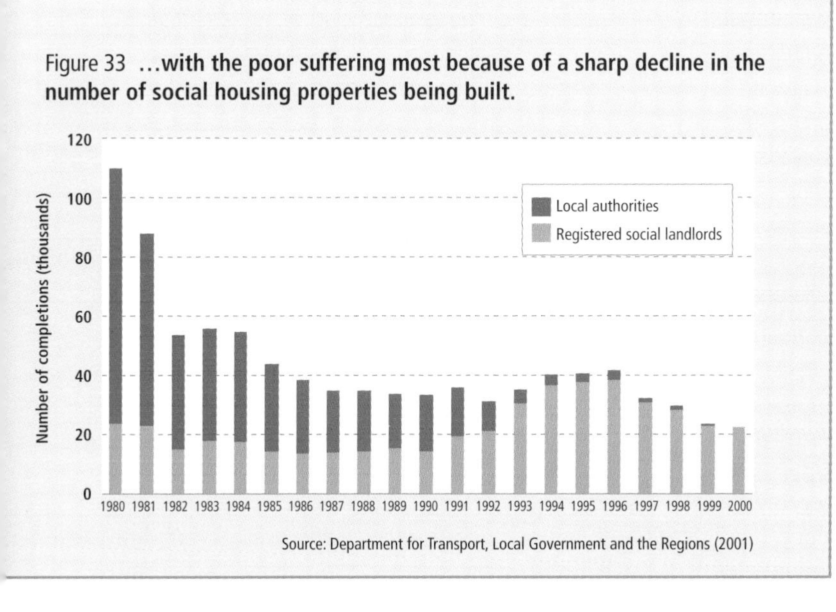

Source: Department for Transport, Local Government and the Regions (2001)

Lack of affordability Even if overall supply were adequate, the most disadvantaged groups cannot afford market prices or rents. The level of subsidy to assist them has fallen steadily in recent years, both 'bricks and mortar' subsidies to those producing affordable homes and, more recently, subsidies to individuals such as Housing Benefit. The total volume of these two kinds of support fell more than 40 per cent in the 1990s. New building of social housing, having halved from 1960 to 1980, continued to diminish rapidly throughout the 1980s and 90s (Figure 33) (Wilcox 2001).

Tackling housing: Facing reality

This report argues that tackling disadvantage in Britain requires improved access not just to adequate incomes but also to other essential resources affecting people's quality of life. Adequate housing is central to a decent lifestyle. It can only be made accessible to everyone through a combination of improving the overall supply and policies that focus on the needs of the poorest groups.

The long-term crises in housing supply described above arise from some fundamental contradictions between society's collective behaviour and aspirations on the one hand, and what is in practice possible on the other. An aspiration for every family to have a decent self-contained home will not in the long term be achievable if everyone wants to live in leafy suburbs or in rural areas – and to prevent others from building nearby. Society's aspiration for homelessness and squalor to become a thing of the past cannot be achieved without the will to create a much more reliable system to ensure that everyone is able to afford a decent home.

Changing perceptions

In facing up to the realities of housing supply and its effect on the nation's well-being, several aspects of the nation's collective attitude need to be addressed:

- The importance to the nation's future health and happiness of a plentiful supply of new homes should be recognised. Shortages harm individuals who cannot afford decent housing, and the whole economy through their inflationary impact.
- The value of urban living should be appreciated. It is simply not practical for everybody to live in the countryside or low-density suburbs, particularly if we wish to limit the need for greenfield building. The solution is not simply to invoke people to live in cities and towns, but to ensure that inner suburbs are attractive to families, and that the centres of conurbations are attractive to those without children.
- It should be accepted that, while brownfield development on urban sites is the best form of new housing, not all of the homes of tomorrow can be built on recycled land. Even if the government's target of 60 per cent of new homes on such sites is met, over 1½ million homes will need to be built on greenfield land in the next two decades. A more reasoned debate is needed about this issue (see box).

Long-term policy goals

- Work to change perceptions about land for housing and about urban living.
- Increase supply, using new approaches.
- Ensure that there is a sufficient supply of affordable homes.

Increasing supply

The need to increase housing supply to meet demand has now been accepted by Government. A range of mechanisms can help this process, in particular:

- Concentrating new development in extensions of existing urban areas. This is more likely to create sustainable communities that plug into existing public transport routes, schools and other facilities than multiple free-standing new developments. Such an approach can be systematically planned with the close involvement of local authorities. Where several hundred homes are involved, there is great scope for negotiating lower land prices to create 'planning gains' that help fund affordable housing and community amenities.
- Putting substantial public and private investment behind attempts to reverse the decline of major urban areas.
- Harnessing private resources in the public interest. The JRF has demonstrated for example how 'City-centre Apartments for Single People at Affordable Rents' (CASPAR) can help revive inner city areas (Joseph Rowntree Foundation web – a).
- A more positive approach to planning. Planning authorities need to take a bold step away from reacting, often negatively, to proposals from

'Greenfield' land: A misunderstanding

The term 'greenfield' is one of the most unfortunate and inappropriate terms used in present policy debate. Contrary to public perception, it does not refer simply to rolling countryside, but to any land that has not been previously developed. Not all of this land is in attractive or environmentally sensitive countryside. Much of it is on the edge of existing cities or towns. A better understanding of this term would help shift a debate away from *whether* to build on such land, to a more rational one about *which* land is most appropriate for new development.

developers. Rather, they must work pro-actively with all interested parties to find ways of meeting housing needs while minimising environmental damage. In developing 'masterplans' that create a framework for the development of an area, they may need to work with intermediaries such as major housing associations, who have expertise in meeting the needs of communities but not a narrow interest in building homes for sale.

Improving affordability

The most important single thing that can be done to enable more low-income households to afford decent housing is to improve supply. As long as it falls far short of demand, making housing affordable will be an uphill struggle, and subsidies to help some groups risk simply displacing others.

Specific measures that make housing affordable to such groups remain essential: the market on its own will never provide guarantees. But this should not mean simply building rented social housing for the poor. The single tenure monolithic housing estate has been a failure: a more sustainable model requires a mixture of tenures and of incomes, in which where you live does not label and stigmatise you.

The present government has promised a welcome reversal of the long-standing decline in public investment in housing. This will have to be sustained, and investment deployed wisely. Three routes to affordability need to be pursued:

- Subsidies for production were the traditional means of producing more affordable homes, with the state footing most of the bill for building social housing. These have been virtually abolished for council housing. Funding for registered social landlords remains at historically modest levels, especially considering rising land, property and building costs.

Reversing decline of urban area: Policy illustrations

- Establish *stronger financial incentives* to reclaim and re-use urban land.
- Revive *higher density residential building*, including high rise, but for better-off households without children rather than poor ones with children, as was tried in the 1960s and 1970s.
- *Redevelop undesirable existing residential areas*, in consultation with residents, to create more attractive communities.
- Create incentives *to re-use empty properties* and to convert outmoded industrial and office buildings.

Figure 34 **Total personal subsidies for housing fell steadily in the 1990s**

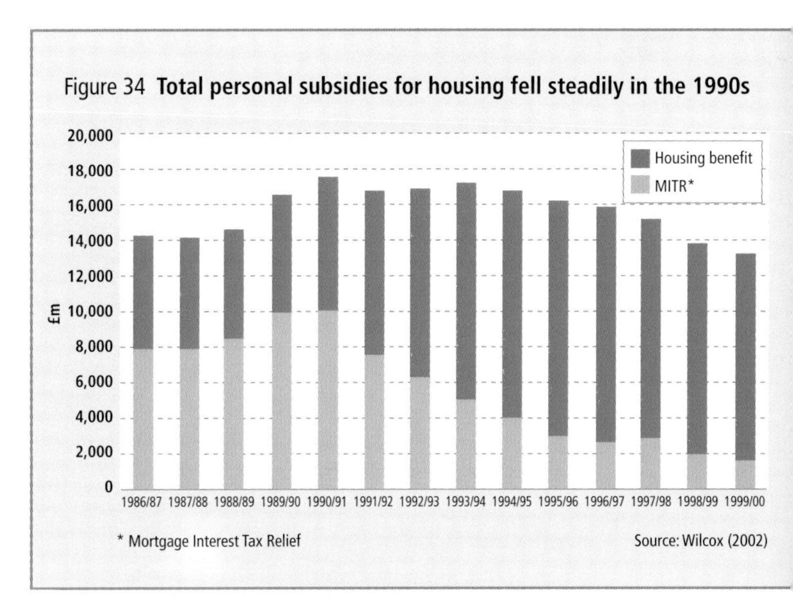

* Mortgage Interest Tax Relief

Source: Wilcox (2002)

Despite new private finance for social housing, there is no substitute for higher levels of public investment.

- Planning gains can help reduce the public cost of affordable housing, requiring landowners (or developers) to divert some of their potential profit into low-rent or low-cost accommodation as a condition for planning consent. This can help create more integrated communities. However, planning gain should not be oversold as a substitute for other measures to promote affordability. It risks being discredited if it holds up development, and remains highly dependent on buoyant market conditions.
- Personal subsidies to help pay for housing have long been the biggest form of housing support. Recently, they have been reduced with the phasing out of mortgage interest tax relief, tougher rules on housing benefit and reductions in unemployment (Figure 34). A more rational support system in the long term would be a universal needs-related housing allowance. In the meantime, existing support needs reforming. Home owners are inadequately protected against loss of income through voluntary mortgage protection insurance: a compulsory scheme would be better. For tenants, the introduction of tax credits for working families has reduced dependency on housing benefit, but in the process exacerbated work disincentives. Better integration, bringing Housing Benefit within the tax credit system, could address this.

6 Long-term care: Meeting the growing demand

Access to care could become a key source of social inequality in later life

Many people still face the prospect of poverty and disadvantage in old age. The drop of income associated with no longer earning is nothing new. But the degree of disadvantage faced by many older people in the future will depend increasingly on the quality, availability and affordability of care. If provision is insufficient, those unable to afford care after the onset of dementia or severe physical impairment will face considerable hardship. Unlike many forms of disadvantage, this risk could affect many who have lived on comfortable incomes for much of their lives, as well as the persistently poor.

Long-term care is likely to become a central aspect of social support in the years ahead – not just a problem affecting the few. One in four people over 85 are in some form of institutional care. People approaching that age face huge uncertainties about their ability to find satisfactory arrangements and about having to use up all their assets to do so, at a time of life when uncertainty is hardest to cope with.

There is already a crisis developing in long-term care provision...

At present, long-term care for those who are unable to afford private provision is supported by social services departments through fees to care homes. This provision has been under increasing pressure, because of:

- rising staffing costs, caused in some areas by the rise in the minimum wage and in others by the need to raise wages because of high general labour demand
- improvements in standards required by the government, in line with rising expectations
- pressure on social services budgets, which are having to spend more than is allocated by central government.

The result is that social services departments are often unable to pay the required fees in full, and many care homes are having to close (Figure 36). Although central government is now providing subsidies to cover the health care cost of those in nursing homes and of 'intermediate care' for people before returning from hospital to their own homes, these have not affected the cost or availability of residential care without a nursing element.

Is less residential care being replaced by more support for people staying in their own homes? Quite the contrary: the number receiving support has declined (Figure 37), although total hours of support have risen. Costs here are also rising, because spending is being concentrated on those needing the greatest care. The risk of this is that those currently requiring low-level care will become more needy, as lack of help may cause their health to deteriorate further.

...and although relatively modest demographic change gives a window of opportunity...

In the United Kingdom, as in other countries, the number of people over 75 and over 85 will rise rapidly over the long term. However, the UK's 'demographic time bomb' is not set to detonate in the next 20 years. While the number over 85 will almost treble by mid-century, the most rapid increase will only begin in the

Long-term care - the problem

Figure 35 **The number of over-85s will rise relatively slowly in the next 20 years...**

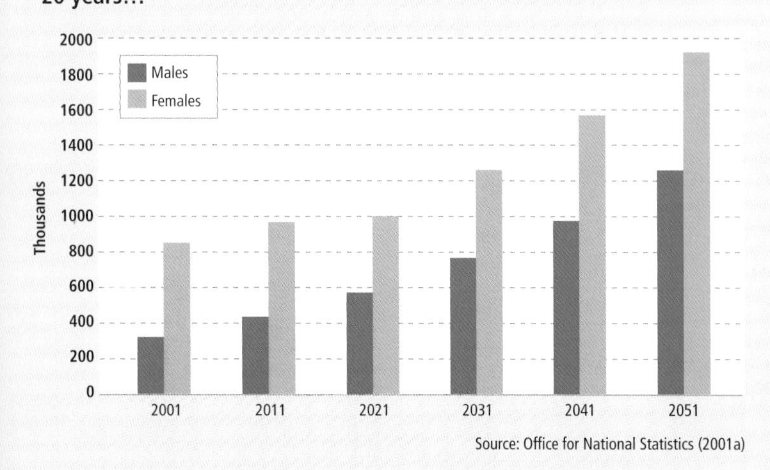

Source: Office for National Statistics (2001a)

Figure 36 **...and problems are already emerging with the closure of care homes...**

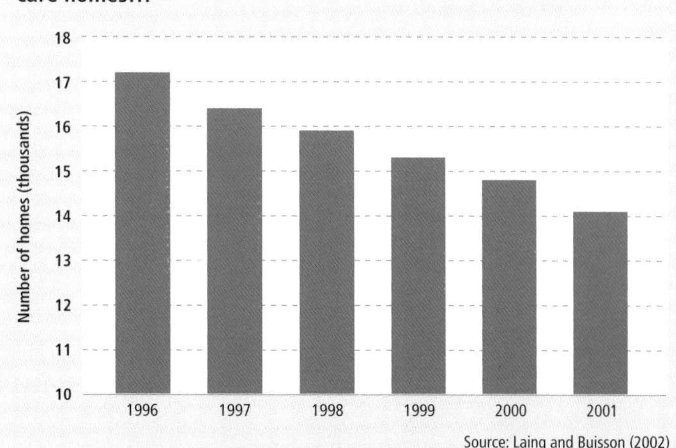

Source: Laing and Buisson (2002)

2020s (Figure 35). Only in the 2030s will the most numerous generations born in the years after World War II start to reach this age (GAD 2002). This gives a 'window of opportunity' to build up provision for long-term care before the most severe rise in demand occurs.

...while medical and technological change could help...

The impact of ageing on demand for long-term care is, in present conditions, dramatic. For example, the incidence of dementia doubles in each five-year age band, affecting 1 in 60 people aged 65, but 1 in 5 people aged over 80. More than 70 per cent of this latter age-group have some form of disability.

It is possible, however, that as lives lengthen, health will improve for any given age-group and the period of morbidity and disability at the end of life will not lengthen greatly. This depends on whether potential breakthroughs in the treatment of conditions such as dementia and Parkinson's disease materialise. This is a real possibility, but remains an area of much uncertainty.

On the other hand, one can predict with more certainty that technology will make it possible to reduce the need for care by helping to sustain independent living. The Joseph Rowntree Foundation has demonstrated that 'smart homes' allow many day-to-day chores to be automated, and for older people's homes to be monitored remotely where needed (Joseph Rowntree Foundation web – b). At the same time, new building regulations require new homes to be built as 'lifetime homes', that are flexible and adaptable, to facilitate independent living for longer (Joseph Rowntree Foundation web – c).

Figure 37 **...while fewer people receive home-based services.**

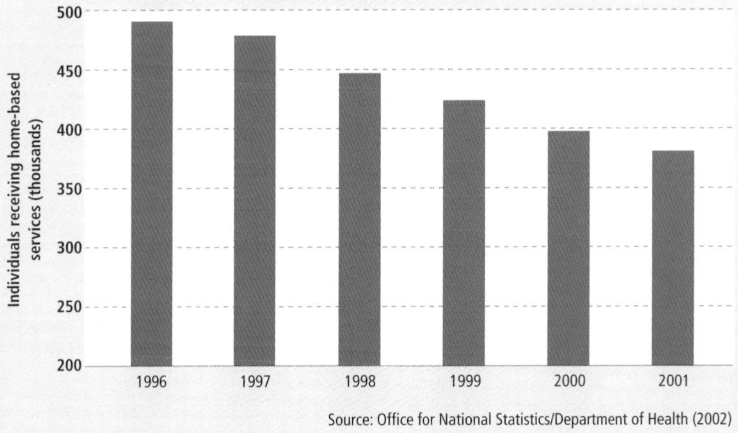

Individuals receiving home-based services (thousands)

500
450
400
350
300
250
200

1996 1997 1998 1999 2000 2001

Source: Office for National Statistics/Department of Health (2002)

...problems with supply threaten to make the situation worse.

While demand for long-term care is therefore not set to explode soon, and even in the long-term could be contained, several factors on the supply side are set to cause further difficulties in the years ahead.

Workforce shortages that are already evident look like being a sign of things to come (Social Services Inspectorate 2000). Staff in this sector have traditionally been poorly paid for highly demanding work, but are now becoming harder to recruit. The only solution to this in the long term is to improve pay, status and training in this sector. Although this will increase costs, there is a growing realisation that essential staff in care support roles must be more highly valued.

Informal care, which has been the mainstay of support, could potentially diminish. At present, over 70 per cent of care is provided on an unpaid basis. However:

- increased mobility means children are more often living further from their parents
- demographic change has increased the number of people of an age where care needs are most common, relative to the number in the age groups that do the most caring
- more women work or have dependent children at a later age
- cultural attitudes to family responsibilities may be changing, while an increase in relationship breakdown creates extra risk of people being left without support.

So far this has not caused a petering out of informal care, but even a small drop in the 70 per cent of care provided informally would require a relatively large percentage increase in paid-for care.

The quality of care will need to be transformed. This process has already started, with a framework for regulation introduced for the first time in the Care Standards Act 2000. However, over the long term, the task of raising standards in line with living standards and expectations should not be underestimated. Attention is needed not just to material standards, including comfort and privacy, but also staff quality, social life and a range of other dimensions which are likely to emerge in the future. Most importantly, care homes need to be able to respond to the demands of their users, who will increasingly expect to enjoy the kind of choice and decent living standards that are available in other areas of modern life.

Tackling long-term care: Contain demand, but face the cost

Like housing, care in old age is a basic need, and those without proper access to it are subject to considerable suffering. Also like housing, the present system creates problems of access for a wide range of people, but the poorest groups suffer most because they have little or no choice. Ensuring universal access to this service, with quality and choice, is therefore now a key aspect of tackling disadvantage.

Potentially, the cost to society of providing for long-term care as the population ages could be enormous. The growth in the next half century of the numbers over 85 needs to be multiplied by the extra unit cost involved in providing high quality domiciliary or residential care for everyone who needs it. Therefore action is needed on two fronts. First, there are things that can be done to contain growth in demand for the most expensive form of care, in residential homes. Second, mechanisms must be found to support the undoubtedly high cost of providing long-term care in a way that makes it accessible to all.

Demand could be contained by health education...

The health of the older population could, over the long term, be improved not just by preventative interventions with people who are already elderly, but also by encouraging younger adults to lead healthier lifestyles. The growing affluence of the population gives more people the resources to afford healthy living, if they make appropriate lifestyle choices. However, the resources to live healthy lives are not distributed equally, and the general assault on disadvantage advocated by this report would have spin-off effects in terms of health-related needs in later life.

...by preventive support...

For older people who might potentially need long-term care, improved low-intensity support would help to prevent or delay the need for it. This is presently a low priority for cash-strapped local authorities, which have been running down traditional home help services. Yet the evidence shows that low-level help, for example with housework, can sustain self-respect and confidence, which itself may help avoid the need for residential care (Joseph Rowntree Foundation 1999).

Long-term policy goals

- Contain the cost by limiting the need for residential care.
- Create a financial mechanism to make high quality care available to all.

...and by intermediate care...

At present, it can be hard to discharge people who do not require close medical attention but do at present need residential care. Intermediate care can provide a temporary solution. This not only reduces expenditure on hospital beds and cuts the number of emergency re-admissions, but can also help prevent the need for permanent admission to residential care. Promisingly, the Government is now investing in such 'intermediate' care. The Joseph Rowntree Housing Trust has demonstrated the scope for such intermediate care – see box.

...but we must face the costs of long-term care.

The lack of a reliable system for financing long-term care has for many older people become a source of worry and led to a sense of injustice. Whether among people dependent on the State who are finding it harder to get the services they need, or among those who have accumulated modest assets and fear they will lose them having to pay the cost of care, there is a

JRHT Intermediate Care

The Joseph Rowntree Housing Trust's (JRHT) Continuing Care Retirement Community has provided an opportunity to see the extent to which residential and nursing care can be used for short periods of 'intermediate care'. The community has a residential care and nursing care centre in the middle of a complex of 150 individual bungalows.

- 29 of the community's 200 bungalow residents spent at least one night in this community's care home over the 12 months to December 2000
- they paid 41 visits to the care home, staying a total of 714 nights.

The JRHT estimates that the availability of this facility within the community saved 374 'bed nights' in hospital last year. The majority of these came from people being discharged from hospital earlier than would have been possible but for the provision of this 'intermediate' care. Others were saved because of provision of short-term nursing care.

sense of a 'broken contract' with the State. Many people have expected the State to provide social care, just like health care, free where it is needed.

In 1996, following its Inquiry into Meeting the Costs of Continuing Care, the Joseph Rowntree Foundation proposed that long-term care should be free at the point of delivery, with a compulsory insurance scheme to cover much of the cost (see box). Three years later, the Royal Commission on Long-Term Care proposed that nursing and personal care – although not accommodation – should become free at the point of delivery but that it should be funded from general taxation.

For most of the UK, the Government has rejected the Commission's recommendations, and decided to fund only the nursing element of long-term care. One of its arguments is that free care would reduce the amount of informal care provided in the home by family and friends. In Scotland, on the other hand, the Scottish Executive has started to fund care as well as nursing costs in 2002. It is estimated that this might raise the total cost of care by about 12 per cent, but abuse of the system could be avoided by strict medical definitions of conditions eligible for personal care.

The JRF believes its earlier recommendation for a regulated, funded and compulsory National Care Insurance scheme is viable, fair and efficient. However, the recommendations, summarised below, are not the only means of creating access to care free at the point of delivery. The important thing is to find some way of paying for care that will give poor as well as rich people access to quality and choice when accessing this essential service. Recent estimates by the Institute for Public Policy Research show that in the next half century neither the total cost of care nor the proportion that needs to be funded publicly are likely to be excessive relative to the nation's resources.

Paying for care: A policy illustration

In 1996, the Joseph Rowntree Foundation published the results of its Inquiry into Meeting the Costs of Continuing Care. It recommended a funded National Care Insurance scheme to pay the nursing and care costs for all who need long-term care. During the coming quarter century, before the rapid increase in the number of people aged over 85, such a scheme could build up funds that would help make it sustainable in future years. A National Care Council would be established to set and review national standards of care entitlements and set levels of contribution rates – making 'in-flight' corrections to these as and when required.

Such a scheme would:

- reduce greatly the costs of insuring against the potentially catastrophic risks of long-term care, because of the universal nature of a national scheme, with administration and marketing costs kept to a minimum and all those in work contributing
- avoid 'free riders' who choose not to make provision assuming that society will feel obliged to pick up the bill for them
- avoid 'cherry picking' by private insurers (which is likely to become more of a problem as genetic testing and other techniques reveal levels of individual risk), by pooling the risks across the whole population
- end anxieties about the loss of assets on the part of those who have saved during their working lives, rewarding those who have made provision for their old age and/or wish to pass on an inheritance to the next generation
- and, most importantly, generate substantial extra resources to supplement the input of the tax payer (who would continue to pay for those whose insurance-based entitlements are insufficient): this would fund more and better care all round.

Contributions to be paid into the scheme recommended by the JRF would be compulsory at a rate which would ensure that someone on average earnings all their life would put in sufficient for insurance cover against the full cost of their continuing care. The Government Actuary assessed this level at 1–1 1/2 per cent of average earnings. The scheme was costed as increasing public expenditure at about £540 million per annum if introduced immediately, before there was any funded element, but £3 billion a year from contributions would be invested in building up a fund for future beneficiaries. Payments out of this fund would be small over the next 20 years, going only to those who have paid in, so that by the early 2020s the fund would be big enough to pay for about half of all continuing care.

Conclusion: A long-term commitment is affordable

Poverty and disadvantage are avoidable...

This report has argued that widespread poverty and disadvantage is a damaging and avoidable feature of twenty-first century Britain. The damage is not only experienced by those directly affected but by the whole of society, not least because of the economic cost of having a large group of people who require expensive support and are unable to achieve their full potential.

A strategy to combat disadvantage therefore needs to start with a concerted effort to help everyone play full economic and social roles. This means enabling individuals to acquire skills and access paid work, but also valuing a wider range of activities, such as unpaid caring, and taking steps to help whole communities to flourish. At the same time, those who are unable to flourish in a market economy require support in a variety of forms.

In a number of areas this requires governments to adopt bold long-term policy objectives. Among the most important ones suggested by this report are:

- a decisive reorienting of the education system to ensure that it serves those who have in the past gained least from it
- measures to allow poorer groups to enjoy a higher than average rate of income growth in the coming years, primarily through better opportunities and more stable and generous support
- a new attitude to housing supply in which society accepts the importance of meeting growing overall demand as well as of expanding provision for those unable to pay market prices
- a system for paying for long-term care that gives everyone access to quality options.

...if they are tackled with persistence and co-ordination...

Of course, none of this can be achieved overnight. Yet if these principles are pursued over a long period, real progress is possible. Critically, this requires persistent, simultaneous action on a range of fronts, where sporadic or disjointed efforts would be ineffective.

One example is the pursuit of policies to enhance the incomes of people with low earnings from work. Efforts to raise productivity, progressive increases in the minimum wage and the use of tax credits to support the most needy families would each, as an isolated policy, encounter serious difficulties. Pursued together, they have a much better chance of succeeding.

Similarly, measures focusing on income enhancement will, over the long term, be more effective if combined with wider measures to improve access to certain things that disadvantaged people need. Improving the overall supply of housing, for example, is a long-term mission that is essential if one is to ensure that people can afford to pay for decent accommodation. With a chronic overall shortage, no policies to supply affordable homes or help people pay their rent will be adequate to eliminate housing disadvantage and associated hardship.

...and over the long term these principles are affordable.

This report has not produced a detailed, costed policy agenda. Instead, it shows, first, that in principle it is possible to tackle relative poverty over 20 years by diverting a relatively small percentage of economic growth to poorer groups. Second, the report argues that a higher proportion of the resources spent on services such as education should be concentrated on tackling disadvantage.

Will this require new money to be raised from the taxpayer? In the case of spending on key services such as education, housing and health, the present government has already committed large increases. The important thing will be to sustain higher spending in these areas and to focus on tackling the problems identified in this report.

For raising the floor of incomes to the level recommended, some new resources may be needed. How much is required over the long term depends on success in raising the capacity of disadvantaged groups to succeed economically. However, three factors make a degree of direct redistributive taxation look like a feasible option.

First, the present government has made a start. The past five years have shown that it is politically possible to have budgets that give disproportionately to poorer groups with some modest extra call on the means of richer ones.

Second, gradual movement in this direction over the long term does not require anyone to have reduced disposable income – simply for some to become better off slightly more slowly.

Third, the UK remains a relatively low taxed country, with most of its EU neighbours raising considerably more, especially in direct taxation.

This is not an argument for making redistributive taxation the centre of a strategy to combat poverty and disadvantage. But alongside the other measures recommended here, it can play its part.

Notes

1 GAD (2002) *2000 based population projections.*

2 See Department for Work and Pensions (2002a).

3 The estimates calculated for this report use the same methods as in Piachaud D. and Sutherland H (2001), Child Poverty: Aims Achievements and Prospects for the future, *New Economy*, 8 (2) pp. 71–6 and in Sutherland H, (2001), 'Five Labour budgets (1997-2001): impacts on the distribution of household incomes and on child poverty', Microsimulation Unit Research Note MU/RN/41. The only difference is that an after housing cost measure is used rather than a before housing cost one.
POLIMOD is based on micro-data from the Family Expenditure Survey. These data are Crown Copyright. They have been made available by the Office for National Statistics (ONS) through the Data Archive and are used by permission. Neither the ONS nor the Data Archive bear any responsibility for the analysis or interpretation of the data reported here.

4 DFES analysis of three waves of the Youth Cohort Study.

5 See for example Turok, I and Edge, N (1999) *The jobs gap in Britain's cities*, Bristol: The Policy Press/JRF.

6 Department for Work and Pensions estimate 2001.

7 HM Treasury *Budget 2002* (Red Book) p. 88; the child portion of the Child Tax Credit is pegged to earnings in the present Parliament.

8 Proposed by the Institute for Public Policy Research (2002) *A new contract for retirement.*

9 A full discussion of the figures and assumptions behind these calculations are contained in Darton and Strelitz (2003).

References

Anadike-Danes, M., Fothergill, S., Glyn, A., Grieve Smith, J., Kitson, M., Martin, R., Rowthorn, R., Turok, I., Tyler, P. and Webster, D. (2001) *Labour's New Regional Policy: An assessment*, Seaford: Regional Studies Association.

Barber, M. (1999) *Minutes of Evidence taken before the Education and Employment Committee* (Education Sub-Committee), 14 July, London: The Stationery Office.

Bate, R., Best, R. and Holmans, A. (2000) *On the Move: The housing consequences of migration*, York: Joseph Rowntree Foundation/YPS.

Bradbury, B. and Janitti, M. (1999) *Child Poverty Across Industrialised Nations*, Innocenti Occasional Papers, EPS 1971, Florence: UNICEF.

Brewer, M., Clark, T. and Goodman, A. (2002) *The Government's Child Poverty Target: How much progress has been made?* London: Institute for Fiscal Studies.

Cambridge Econometrics (2002) *Regional Economic Prospects 2015*, Cambridge: Cambridge Econometrics.

Centre for Economic Performance (2002) *State of Working Britain Update*, London: Centre for Economic Performance, London School of Economics.

Clark, J., Dyson, A. and Millward, A. (1999) *Housing and Schooling: A case-study in joined-up problems*, York: Joseph Rowntree Foundation/YPS.

Danziger, S. and Waldfogel, J. (2000) *Investing in Children: What do we know? What should we do?* CASE paper 34, London: Centre for the Analysis of Social Exclusion, London School of Economics.

Darton, D. and Strelitz, J. (eds) (2003) *Tackling UK Poverty and Disadvantage in the Twenty-First Century: An exploration of the issues*, <http://www.jrf.org.uk/bookshop/ebooks/1859350909.pdf>.

Department for Education and Employment (1999) *Report of Policy Action Team 1: Jobs for All*, Nottingham: DfEE

Department for Education and Skills (2001) *Youth Cohort Study: The activities and experiences of 16-year-olds: England and Wales 2000*, <http://www.dfes.gov.uk/statistics/DB/SFR/s0230/index.html> Accessed 27 January 2003.

Department for Education and Skills (2002) *Participation in Education and Training by 16- and 17-year-olds in each local area in England 1998 to 2000*, <http://www.dfes.gov.uk/statistics/DB/SBU/b0369/index.html> Accessed 27 January 2003.

Department for Transport, Local Government and the Regions (2001) *Housing Statistics 2001*, London: The Stationery Office.

Department for Work and Pensions (2002a) *Households Below Average Income – 1994/5 to 2000/01*, London: The Stationery Office.

Department for Work and Pensions (2002b) *The Abstract of Statistics*, London: The Stationery Office.

Department of Health (2001) *Community Care Statistics 2000/1: Home help/home care services, England*, London: Department of Health.

Dickens, R., Gregg, P. and Wadsworth, J. (2001) 'Non-working classes', *Centrepiece*, Summer, London: Centre for Economic Performance, LSE.

Egan, Sir John (Chair) (1998) *Rethinking Construction: The report of the Construction Task Force*, London: Department of Trade and Industry.

Forster, M. (2000) *Trends and Driving Factors in Income Inequality and Poverty in the OECD Area*, OECD Labour Market and Social Policy Occasional Paper No. 42, Paris, OECD.

GAD (2002) Various documents on site, <http://www.gad.gov.uk/publications/demography-and-statistics.htm> Accessed 27 January 2003.

Gibbons, S. and Machin, S. (2001) *Valuing Primary Schools*, London: Centre for the Economics of Education, London School of Economics.

Gordon, D. and Pantazis, C. (eds) (1997) *Breadline Britain in the 1990s*, Aldershot: Ashgate Publishing Ltd.

Gordon, D., Adelman, L., Ashworth, K., Bradshaw, J., Levitas, R., Middleton, S., Pantazis, C., Patsios, D., Payne, S., Townsend, P., and Williams, J. (2000) *Poverty and Social Exclusion in Britain*, York: Joseph Rowntree Foundation.

Gregg, P., Harkness, S. and Machin, S. (1999) *Child Development and Family Income*. York: Joseph Rowntree Foundation/YPS.

Hallgarten, J. (2001) 'School league tables: Have they outlived their usefulness?' *New Economy*, 8 (4), 189–96.

Hicks, J. and Allen, G. (1999) *A Century of Change: Trends in UK statistics since 1900*, London: House of Commons Library.

HM Treasury/Department of Trade and Industry (2001) *Productivity in the UK: The regional dimension*, London: The Stationery Office.

HM Treasury (2002) *Budget 2002*, London: The Stationery Office.

Hobcraft, J. and Kiernan, K. (1999) *Childhood poverty, early motherhood and adult social exclusion*, CASE Paper 28, London: Centre for the Analysis of Social Exclusion, London School of Economics.

Home Office (2000) *The 2000 British Crime Survey: England and Wales*, London: Home Office.

Index of Multiple Deprivation (2003) *Indices of deprivation*, <http://www.urban.odpm.gov.uk/research/id2000/>. Accessed 27 January 2003.

Institute for Employment Research (2001) *Projections of Occupations and Qualifications 2000/2001*, Sheffield: DfEE.

Institute for Fiscal Studies (2002) *Fiscal Facts*, <http://www.ifs.org.uk/taxsystem/contents.shtml> Accessed 27 January 2003.

Jefferson, C.W. and Trainor, M. (1996) 'Public sector relocation and regional development', *Urban Studies*, 33 (1), 37–48.

Joseph Rowntree Foundation (web – a) 'CASPAR Developments', <http://www.jrf.org.uk/housingandcare/caspar/> Accessed 6 January 2003.

Joseph Rowntree Foundation (web – b) 'Smart Homes', <http://www.jrf.org.uk/housingandcare/smarthomes/> Accessed 6 January 2003.

Joseph Rowntree Foundation (web – c) 'Lifetime Homes', <http://www.jrf.org.uk/housingandcare/lifetimehomes/> Accessed 6 January 2003.

Joseph Rowntree Foundation (1999) 'Low intensity support: Preventing dependency', *Foundations* 159.

Joseph Rowntree Foundation (2000) 'Exclusive countryside? Social inclusion and regeneration in rural areas', *Foundations* 760.

Kempson, E. (1996) *Life on a Low Income*, York: Joseph Rowntree Foundation/YPS.

Laing & Buissson Ltd (2002) *Care of Elderly People UK Market Survey 2002*, London: Laing & Buisson Ltd.

Latham, Sir Michael (1994) *Constructing the Team: Final report of the government/industry review of procurement and contractual arrangements in the UK construction industry*, London: HMSO.

Mack, J. and Lansley, S. (1983) *Breadline Britain*, London: Allen & Unwin.

Meltzer, H. and Gatward, R. (2000) *Mental Health of Children and Adolescents in Great Britain*, London: Office for National Statistics.

Molnar, A., Smith, P., Zahorik, J., Palmer, A., Halbach, A. and Ehrle, K. (1999) 'Evaluating the SAGE program: A pilot program in targeted pupil-teacher reduction in Wisconsin', *Educational Evaluation and Policy Analysis*, 21 (2), 165–77.

National Literacy Trust (1995) OFSTED research and analysis cited by National Literacy Trust, <http://www.literacytrust.org.uk/Database/stats/poorexam.html> Accessed 24 January 2003.

National Statistics (2002) *Nomis*, <http://www.nomisweb.co.uk> Accessed November 2002. Site moved January 2003 to <http://parus.dur.ac.uk/>.

Nickell, S. (2002) 'The assessment: The economic record of the Labour Government since 1997', *Oxford Review of Economic Policy*, 18 (2).

O'Connell, P.J. (1999) *Adults in Training: An international comparison of continuing training and education*, Working Paper CERI/WD (99) 1, Paris: OECD.

OECD (1996) *Employment Outlook*, Paris: Organization for Economic Cooperation and Development.

OECD (1997) *Literacy Skills for the Knowledge Society*, Paris: Organization for Economic Cooperation and Development.

OECD (1998) *Education at a Glance*, Paris: OECD.

OECD (2001) *Knowledge and Skills for Life: First results from PISA 2000*, Paris: OECD.

Office for National Statistics (1990) *New Earnings Survey*, London: The Stationery Office.

Office for National Statistics (2000) *Social Trends 30*, London: The Stationery Office.

Office for National Statistics (2001a) *Social Trends*, London: The Stationery Office.

Office for National Statistics (2001b) *Regional Trends 2001*, London: The Stationery Office.

Office for National Statistics (2001c) *New Earnings Survey*, London: The Stationery Office.

Office for National Statistics (2002) *Social Trends 32*, London: The Stationery Office.

Office for National Statistics/Department of Health (2002) *Community Care Statistics 2001: Home help/home care services*, London: The Stationery Office.

Office of the Deputy Prime Minister (2002) *Housing Statistics 2002*, London: The Stationery Office.

Parker, H. (ed.) (1998) *Low Cost but Acceptable: A minimum income standard for the UK – Families with young children*, Bristol: The Policy Press.

Rahman, M., Palmer, G. and Kenway, P. (2001) *Monitoring Poverty and Social Exclusion 2001*, York: Joseph Rowntree Foundation.

Robertson, D. and Symons, J. (1996) 'Do peer groups matter? Peer groups versus schooling effects on academic attainment', *CEP 311*, Centre for Economic Performance, London School of Economics.

Robinson, P. (1997) *Literacy, numeracy and economic performance*, London: Centre for Economic Performance, London School of Economics.

Social Services Inspectorate (2000) *Modern Social Services: A commitment to people. The Ninth Annual Report of the Chief Inspector of Social Services*, London: Department of Health.

Sunley, P., Martin, R. and Nativel, C. (2001) 'Mapping the New Deal: Local disparities in the performance of Welfare-to-Work', *Transactions of the Institute of British Geographers*, 26 (4), 484–512.

Wilcox, S. (2001) *Housing Finance Review 2001/02*, Coventry: Chartered Institute of Housing; London: Council of Mortgage Lenders.

Wilcox, S. (2002) *UK Housing Review 2002/03*, Coventry: Chartered Institute of Housing; London: Council of Mortgage Lenders.

People consulted by JRF

The Joseph Rowntree Foundation and the authors of this report would like to thank the following for contributing their knowledge and views during the course of this project. Responsibility for the content of this report remains fully with the authors.

John Adams, IPPR
John Adcock, Freelance Writer
Mal Ainscow, Manchester University, and government adviser
Stephen Aldridge, Cabinet Office
Tony Atkinson, Cambridge University
Mog Ball, Consultant
Sir Peter Barclay CBE
Ian Basnett, Camden & Islington Health Authority
David Bell, Stirling University
Jamie Bell, CBI
Fran Bennett, University of Oxford
Richard Berthoud, University of Essex
Rodney Bickerstaffe, National Pensioners Convention
Mark Beatson, DTI
Dame Margaret Booth DBE, JRF Trustee
Dame Ann Bowtell DCB, JRF Trustee
Jonathan Bradshaw, University of York
Don Brand, National Institute for Social Work
Mike Brewer, IFS
Richard Brooks, IPPR
Peter Bunn, DTI
Tania Burchardt, London School of Economics
Paul Burstow MP
Jabeer Butt, REU
Michael Carley, Heriot-Watt University
Karen Chouhan, De Montfort University
Dame June Clark DBE, University of Wales
George Cowcher, One North East
Diane Coyle, The Independent
John Crook, Department of Health
Gillian Dalley, Centre for Policy on Ageing
Shirley Dex, Cambridge University
Paula Diggle, HM Treasury
Andrew Dilnot CBE, Institute of Fiscal Studies
Josie Dixon, Improvement and Development Agency
Kenneth Dixon CBE DL, JRF Trustee, Chair
Danny Dorling, University of Leeds
Tim Dwelly, Consultant
Alan Dyson, Newcastle University
Rebecca Endean, DWP
Lord Filkin
Janet Ford, York University
Julie Fry, Treasury
David Gilborn, Institute of Education
Sir Alistair Graham, Policy Complaints Authority
Catherine Graham-Harrison, JRF Trustee
Anne Green, University of Warwick
Ruth Hancock, University of Leicester
David Harbourne, North Yorkshire LSC
Tessa Harding, Help the Aged
David Hargreaves, Government education adviser
Susan V Hartshorne, JRF Trustee
Helena Herklots, Age Concern England
Peter Hetherington, The Guardian
John Hills, London School of Economics
Gina Hocking, Consultant
Nicholas Holgate, Treasury
Marilyn Howard, Consultant
John Hubbard, DfES
John Humphries, DTI
Lord Joffe CBE
Savita Katbamna, University of Leicester
Elaine Kempson, Bristol University
Kathleen Kiernan, London School of Economics
Alex Kirwan, DfES
John Knell, Industrial Society
William Laing, Laing & Buisson Ltd
Janice Lawson, DfES
Desmond Le Grys, Consultant
Bob Lewis, Continuing Care Conference
Richard McCarthy, Peabody Trust
James McCormick, Scottish Council Foundation
John McCracken, Department of Health
Rob MacDonald, Teesside University
Duncan Maclennan, Glasgow University
Mary MacLeod, National Family & Parenting Institute
Hamish McRae, The Independent
Mary Marshall, Stirling University
Glyn Mathias
Barbara Maughan, Institute of Psychiatry
Robert Maxwell CVO CBE, JRF Trustee
Pamela Meadows, JRF Adviser
Paul Medlicott, Consultant
Jonathan Michie, Birkbeck College
Sue Middleton, Loughborough University
Jane Millar, University of Bath
Heidi Mirza, Middlesex University
Jenny Morris
Michael Moynagh, The Tomorrow Project
Sarah Mulley, Treasury
Daniel Murphy, Inland Revenue
Nigel Naish, JRF Trustee
Gus O'Donnell, Treasury
Derek Osborn, Consultant
Carey Oppenheim, No 10 Policy Unit
Debby Ounsted, JRF Trustee
Michael Parkinson, John Moores University
Theresa Perchaud and colleagues, NACAB
Norman Perry, Housing Corporation
Chris Pond MP
Claire Rayner
Sue Regan, IPPR
Ceridwen Roberts
David Robinson, Community Links
Janice Robinson, King's Fund Centre
Angela Sarkis, Social Exclusion Unit
Tom Schuller, Birkbeck College
Martin Shreeve
Mark Shucksmith, University of Aberdeen
Gurbux Singh
George Smith, University of Oxford
Rob Smith, Regional Co-ordination Unit
Daphne Statham, National Institute for Social Work
Keith Summer, Centre for Policy on Ageing
Holly Sutherland, University of Cambridge
Lord Sutherland of Houndwood Kt, University of Edinburgh
Nick Timmins, Financial Times
Sir William Utting CB, JRF Trustee, Deputy Chair
Moira Wallace, Social Exclusion Unit
Michael Ward, London Development Agency
Robin Wendt CBE
Michael White, Policy Studies Institute
Christine Whitehead, University of Cambridge
Michael Willmott, Future Foundation
Brian Wilson, Countryside Agency
Gerald Wistow, Nuffield Institute for Health
Raphael Wittenberg, Department of Health